White Slaves of Maquinna

John R. Jewitt's Narrative of Capture and Confinement at Nootka

VICTORIA • VANCOUVER • CALGARY

Heritage House Publishing Co. Ltd.
heritagehouse.ca

Cover design: Nancy St.Gelais
Interior design: Cara Patik
Editing: Cara Patik

Library and Archives Canada Cataloguing in Publication
Jewitt, John R. (John Rodgers), 1783–1821.
    White slaves of Maquinna

    Previous ed. has title: White slaves of the Nootka.
    Includes bibliographical references and index.
    ISBN 978-1-894384-02-5

    1. Jewitt, John R. (John Rodgers), 1783–1821.
    2. Indian captivities—British Columbia.
    3. Nootka Indians.
    I. Title.
    II. Title: White slaves of the Nootka.
    E99.N85J49 2000   971.1'2004979   C00-910040-7

Heritage House acknowledges the financial support for its publishing program from the
Government of Canada through the Canada Book Fund (CBF), Canada Council for the
Arts and the province of British Columbia through the British Columbia Arts Council
and the Book Publishing Tax Credit.

21 20 19 6 7 8

Printed in Canada

A

NARRATIVE

OF THE

ADVENTURES AND SUFFERINGS

OF

JOHN R. JEWITT;

ONLY SURVIVOR OF THE CREW OF THE

SHIP BOSTON,

DURING A CAPTIVITY OF NEARLY THREE YEST AMONG THE SAVAGES OF

NOOTKA SOUND:

WITH AN ACCOUNT OF THE

MANNERS, MODE OF LIVING, AND RELIGIOUS

OPINIONS OF THE NATIVES.

EMBELLISHED WITH A PLATE, REPRESENTING THE SHIP IN
POSSESION OF THE SAVAGES.

"Dire scenes of horror on a savage shore,
"In which, a witness sad, a part I bore"

MIDDLETOWN:
PRINTED BY BETH RICHARDS

1815.

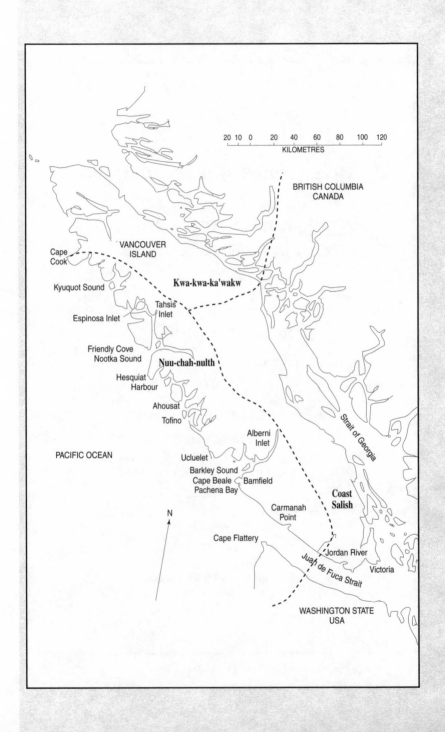

contents

Introduction

to the Heritage House edition

John R. Jewitt's story of capture and slavery at the hands of Maquinna, the great chief of the Mowachaht people, is almost two centuries old. At least 23 editions of the narrative have appeared since it was first published in 1815.

In 1987 Heritage House published a version of the Jewitt narrative called *White Slaves of the Nootka*. This new edition has undergone a name change—to *White Slaves of Maquinna*—for several reasons. The term Nootka is no longer the preferred name for the Nuu-chah-nulth people of Vancouver Island's west coast. Also, the two sailors were held as slaves by Maquinna and a single Mowachaht village rather than by the Nuu-chah-nulth, a term that embraces many different groups of West Coast aboriginal people. To be even more accurate, although John Jewitt and his older ally John Thompson performed tasks for the whole tribe, it was Maquinna's expectations of their usefulness that allowed these two men to live, contrary to the wishes of the Mowachaht warriors who would rather have seen them as dead as their shipmates on the ill-fated *Boston*.

Jewitt's account of his time with the Mowachaht is deserving of its historic popularity. It is both an entertaining adventure tale of survival and a rare source of information on the aboriginal societies on the Northwest Coast. Furthermore, it is an ideal basis of discussion for anyone interested in history as a discipline. The reader must be aware of the discrepancies that Jewitt included, either consciously or unconsciously, in his account. For example, the circumstances of Jewitt's marriage to a Mowachaht woman of his choice, apparently coerced by Maquinna on penalty of death, may raise a few eyebrows. In Nuu-chah-nulth tradition, the parents of the suitor would approach the young girl's parents and negotiate a marriage on their son's behalf. Maquinna assumed this paternal role. Evidently the two men had become friendly enough for Jewitt to be treated like a son. And although Jewitt claimed to detest the forced marriage, his discontent ebbed long enough for him to father a child with the woman.

Jewitt's story is not an objective study of Maquinna's people, their customs, or their motivations. It is a personal narrative and hence extremely subjective. It may also be confused by Jewitt's ambivalence about his master. Jewitt describes two distinct emotional states during his capture. He does not hesitate to maintain that Maquinna was a merciful and kind man. At other times he professes great despair over his circumstances. Some of these emotional inconsistencies might be the work of Jewitt's ghostwriter, Richard Alsop, who may have taken certain fictional liberties with the tale.

Naturally the text is riddled with terms and perceptions that reflect the values of a different era. However, for anyone interested in examining attitudes of the time, this account is indispensable. Jewitt even enlightens the reader with admissions not often made by Europeans. He saw the Nuu-chah-nulth as far from a godless people, instead depicting them as spiritual and devout, believing in one god, *Quahootze*. Also, he disputes common lore regarding the wanton sexuality of Native women. Jewitt states that women slaves of the Nuu-chah-nulth most often performed this duty quite against their will, contrary to the beliefs of merchant sailors.

Jewitt sheds significant light on the practice of slavery among West Coast aboriginals. Nuu-chah-nulth society was hierarchical in nature. Slaves were brought back by the victors from wars, the rightful property of those who had captured them. Such was the fate of Jewitt and Thompson. History shows that these were not the first white men to become slaves to a Nuu-chah-nulth chief. One seaman, John MacKay, who was left by his captain to record the general practices of the local Natives almost two decades before Jewitt's ordeal, became a slave after offending the *maquinna*. He was later rescued in 1787, all of his journals having been destroyed.

There is little known about Jewitt's companion, John Thompson, aside from what is written in the *Narrative*. Jewitt saved his life, but no bond grew while they lived together for the better part of their term of slavery. Thompson never got over his hatred of the Nuu-chah-nulth and would have killed them rather than look at them in return for their treatment of his shipmates.

Was Maquinna justified in his revenge upon the crew of the *Boston*, which led to the captivity of Jewitt and Thompson? Maquinna claimed to have been mistreated over the years by various European captains who came to the cove to trade, and the insults of the captain of the *Boston* simply proved too much to bear. There were more incidents demeaning to Maquinna's dignity than those reported in the *Narrative*. A crewman of the *Harman*, which was reportedly the first fur trading vessel to enter Nootka Sound, lit gunpowder under the seat of Maquinna, an act that proved almost fatal to the chief. And one of his greatest friends and a fellow chief, Callicum, was shot while protesting the Spanish occupation of Nootka Sound in 1789. In short, Maquinna had been spurred to action ever since Europeans arrived in Nootka Sound.

Until that first contact, current theories suggest, the Northwest Coast was populated by people who had crossed the Bering Strait about 12,000 years ago. Archaeological findings suggest that the Mowachaht have populated Yuquot for over 4,200 years. The territory of the Nuu-chah-nulth (whose name means "all along the mountains") runs from the northern part of western

The launching of the *Northwest America* in 1788 signalled the beginning of English occupation of Nootka Sound. This was the first ship built on the Northwest Coast.

Vancouver Island along the coast to the western tip of the Olympic Peninsula in Washington State. The Nuu-chah-nulth are one of about 25 members of the Wakashan language family who all came to be known as the Nootka.

The "discovery" of Nootka Sound was supposedly the first European involvement with Vancouver Island and the Nuu-chah-nulth. In fact, historians studying the trading activities of nomadic tribes have concluded that European settlement occurring far away had already affected the coast peoples by the time Juan Perez sailed into Nootka Sound in 1774. Perez was not much of an influence in any case. He refused to disembark, thinking that the welcoming canoes of the aboriginals were a trap.

That Perez was the first foreigner to come close to Nootka Sound is open to debate. John Meares, a British ship captain sent to consolidate British presence in the area after Captain Cook's departure, stated in his *Voyages made in the years 1778 and 1789, from China to the North West Coast of America* (London 1790) that the Mowachaht told him that their ancestors had met a man in a copper canoe who possessed numerous metal things. However, it is difficult to evaluate the accuracy of such a story.

The first documented account of European presence in Nootka Sound took place on March 30, 1778, when Captain James

Cook claimed the area on behalf of the British. He had stopped in what he called King George's Sound while looking for fresh water, and ended up remaining there for a month.

It was on this visit that the area known as Nootka Sound was named. Once they had decided that Cook and his crew were friendly (and after also mistaking them for salmon transformed into humans), the Nuu-chah-nulth people told them to go around the harbour to Yuquot, which was their name for Nootka Sound, meaning "the place that is hit by winds from all directions." Cook heard their directions as *Nootka, Itchme Nootka, Itchme*. He decided to name the area Nootka rather than King George's Sound, to honour the aboriginal name. The British also applied this name to the 1,500 Mowachaht, "people of the deer," who had villages in this area. Maquinna was also a word misunderstood by Cook. The Mowachaht name for their most prominent chief is *maquinna*.

Cook arrived in 1778, beginning the era of busy fur trade for Nootka Sound—and a controversy over rights to the area that would almost start a world war.

In his ship's log Cook noted the great wealth that could be gained at Nootka. He described the richness of the trade that took place between his crew and the Mowachaht, who would trade anything for metals:

> A great many canoes filled with the Natives were about the ships all day, and a trade commenced betwixt us and them, which was carried on the strictest honisty on boath sides. Their articles were the Skins of various animals, such as Bears, Wolfs, Foxes, Dear, Rackoons, Polecats, Martins and in particular the Sea Beaver, the same as is found on the coast of Kamtchatcka.

The sea otter pelts that he mentions sold in Macao for $10,000, and after Cook published his *A Voyage to the Pacific Ocean* in London, the prospect of rich furs attracted traders from all over the world. Yuquot became the primary port of call for many of these traders, and a fur-trading establishment was set up north of the sound. According to records at the Maritime Museum of British Columbia, in the nineteenth century these pelts would be sold abroad in London for $300 each.

From 1785 to 1794, Britain sent 25 trading ships to Nootka Sound. At first the aboriginals rarely got a fair price for the furs. In the late 1780s, American captain John Kendrick traded $100 worth of goods for pelts that would bring him over $8,000. However, as aboriginals grew familiar with European trading practices, they developed a system of middlemen who would buy (or steal) furs from other tribes and charge a higher price.

As trade increased, claim to Nootka Sound became a bone of contention. In that sense, visitors to Nootka came with either a political agenda or purely economic motivations. In 1788 the British sent Captain John Meares to Yuquot, where he built a hut and a sloop, the *Northwest America*, so that English presence in the area would be noticed by other foreigners. On leaving for a short journey, he said that he intended on his return to purchase the land from Maquinna. However, it is hard to believe the word of a man who history would prove to have falsely claimed "discovery" of the Strait of Juan de Fuca after stealing the journals of Captain Charles W. Barkley.

Martinez, in 1789, in the act of taking over a British ship, the *Argonaut*. The *Argonaut*'s crew had intended to set up a fur factory for the British.

The resulting tension between the British and the Spanish over occupation of the area culminated in the Nootka Convention, which Captain George Vancouver (lower left) helped institute. Stained glass windows in the Friendly Cove church commemorate the event (lower right).

The Spanish, who had claimed the New World for Spain in 1492, sent Don Esteban Jose Martinez to Nootka Sound to settle the area and discourage any other country's infiltration. Unlike the British and other interested nations (i.e., Russia), the Spanish were not interested in trade. They only wanted to ensure that the territory was not occupied by anyone but themselves. When they arrived, they arrested Captain William Douglas, who was left in charge in Meares' absence, and then set up Fort San Miguel. When the Spanish confiscated British ships that were in the area, the "Nootka Controversy" began. In 1790, an attempt at conciliation gave free access to economically attractive areas not populated by Europeans. The Nootka Convention was signed, ceding the land to the British, and two years later George Vancouver and the then governor of Nootka Sound, Don Juan Francisco de la Bodega y Quadra, attempted to institute its decrees but could not agree about anything. The affair was not fully worked out until 1795.

Yuquot (Friendly Cove) became the most important port north of Mexico, but this was not a good thing for the original inhabitants. Historians debate the mortality rates that resulted from European presence on the Northwest Coast, but some suggest that between 1774 and 1874 the aboriginal population decreased from 200,000 to roughly 40,000, a result of disease and increased violence among Native groups.

The virtual disappearance of the sea otter within 40 years of Cook's first visit (in 1911 the species was declared endangered), followed by the establishment of Victoria as a Hudson's Bay Company fort left Nootka Sound a mere shadow of the commercial centre it had been. The Nuu-chah-nulth continued to fight among themselves. In 1881 the West Coast Agency of Indian Affairs was set up. It ensured that aboriginals were reserved some land, albeit a small amount, but no treaties were signed for the area.

The forest industry now seeks the rich resources of Nootka Sound and surrounding areas. In 1914 this industry began to expand as a result of a successful development in the transportation of logs between Victoria and Vancouver. In 1938 the first sawmill was built in the area, and Tahsis saw the birth

Friendly Cove in the 1920s, after lumber rather than furs became its chief attraction. Generations earlier, this site saw the birth of the Nuu-chah-nulth style of whaling.

of Pacific Forest Products Limited. In recent years, land in Nuu-chah-nulth territory has been among the most hotly disputed areas in the debate between logging companies and environmental groups. Meares Island has been a focus for many discussions regarding logging policies.

The twentieth century has brought economic strife to the Mowachaht. Because of its small numbers, the band was assigned only four hectares of land on Nootka Island by the Agency of Indian Affairs. When the population grew, band members had nowhere to go except off the reservation. Almost no Mowachaht remain on Nootka Island. However, Native people everywhere are confident that their cultures are beginning to experience a revival. Many Mowachaht are now involved in the tourism industry at Friendly Cove, where outdoor adventurers explore the history and beauty of Nootka Sound.

This is the place where a young man named John Jewitt came aboard the American trading ship *Boston*, and this is his story of two years spent among a fascinating people in a remote corner of the Pacific Ocean.

NOTE ON THE HERITAGE HOUSE EDITION

Jewitt's original narrative has been edited into chapters, with
wording and punctuation modernized. Readers may find that the
spelling of aboriginal words and names varies from edition to
edition, and that the words seem impossible to pronounce. This
is because English and the language of the Nuu-chah-nulth are
much too different for more than a rough transcription of the
Native language without the use of the phonetic alphabet.

one

Jewitt's Youth

I was born in Boston, a considerable borough town in Lincolnshire, in Great Britain, on the 21st of May 1783. My father, Edward Jewitt, was by trade a blacksmith and esteemed among the first in his line of business in that place. At the age of three years I had the misfortune to lose my mother, a most excellent woman. She died in child-bed, leaving an infant daughter who, with myself and an elder brother by a former marriage of my father, constituted the whole of our family.

My father, who considered a good education as the greatest blessing he could bestow on his children, was very particular in paying every attention to us in that respect, always exhorting us to behave well, and endeavouring to impress on our minds the principles of virtue and morality. No expense in his power was spared to have us instructed in whatever might render us useful and respectable in society.

My brother, who was four years older than myself and of a more hardy constitution, was destined for his own trade. To me my father had resolved to give an education superior to that which is to be obtained in a common school, it being his intention that I should adopt one of the learned professions. Accordingly, at the age of twelve he took me from the school in which I had been taught the first rudiments of learning and placed me under the care of Mr. Moses, a celebrated teacher of an academy at Donnington, about twenty miles from Boston, in order to be instructed in the Latin language and in some of the higher branches of the Mathematics. I there made considerable proficiency in writing, reading, and arithmetic, and obtained a pretty good knowledge of navigation and of surveying. But my progress in Latin was slow, not only owing to the little inclination I felt for learning that language, but to a natural impediment in my speech which rendered it extremely difficult for me to pronounce it. In a short time, with my father's consent, I wholly relinquished the study.

The period of my stay at this place was the most happy of my life. My preceptor, Mr. Moses, was not only a learned but a virtuous, benevolent, and amiable man, universally beloved by his pupils, who took delight in his instruction, and to whom he allowed every proper amusement that consisted with attention to their studies.

One of the principal pleasures I enjoyed was in attending the fair, which is regularly held twice a year at Donnington, in the spring and in the fall; the second day being wholly devoted to selling horses, a prodigious number of which are brought thither for that purpose. As the scholars on these occasions were always indulged with a holiday, I cannot express with what eagerness of youthful expectation I used to anticipate these fairs, nor what delight I felt at the various shows, exhibitions of wild beasts, and other entertainments that they presented. I was frequently visited by my father, who always discovered much joy on seeing me, praised me for my acquirements, and usually left me a small sum for my pocket expenses.

Among the scholars at this academy was one named Charles
Rice with whom I formed a particular intimacy which continued
during the whole of my stay. He was my class and room mate and
as the town he came from, Ashby, was more than 60 miles off,
instead of returning home he used frequently during the vacation
to go with me to Boston. Here he always met with a cordial
welcome from my father, who received me on these occasions
with the greatest affection, apparently taking much pride in me.
My friend, in return, used to take me with him to an uncle of his
in Donnington, a very wealthy man who, having no children of

John Jewitt, as he appeared after his return to
Boston. The book in his hands is probably his
Narrative.

his own, was very fond of his nephew. On his account I was always a welcome visitor at the house.

I had a good voice, and an ear for music, to which I was always passionately attached, though my father endeavoured to discourage this propensity, considering it but an introduction to a life of idleness and dissipation. Having been remarked for my singing at church, which was regularly attended on Sundays and Festival days by the scholars, Mr. Morthrop, my friend Rice's uncle, used frequently to request me to sing. He was always pleased with my exhibitions of this kind and it was no doubt one of the means that secured me so gracious a reception at his house. A number of other gentlemen in the place would sometimes send for me to sing at their houses. As I was not a little vain of my vocal powers, I was much gratified on receiving these invitations, and accepted them with the greatest pleasure.

Thus passed away the two happiest years of my life. Then my father, thinking that I had received a sufficient education for the profession he intended for me, took me from school at Donnington in order to apprentice me to Doctor Mason, a surgeon of eminence at Reasby in the neighbourhood of the celebrated Sir Joseph Banks. With regret did I part from my school acquaintance, particularly my friend Rice, and returned home with my father on a short visit to my family preparatory to my intended apprenticeship. The disinclination I ever had felt for the profession my father wished me to pursue was still further increased on my return. When a child, I was always fond of being in the shop among the workmen, endeavouring to imitate what I saw them do. This disposition so far increased after my leaving the academy that I could not bear to hear the least mention made of my being apprenticed to a surgeon.

I used so many entreaties with my father to persuade him to give up this plan and learn me his own trade that he at last consented. More fortunate would it probably have been for me had I gratified the wishes of this affectionate parent in adopting the profession he had chosen for me, than thus induced him to sacrifice them to mine. However it might have been, I was at length introduced into the shop. My natural turn of mind corresponding with the employment, I became in a short time uncommonly expert at the work to which I was set. I now felt myself well contented, pleased with my occupation and treated with much affection by my father and kindness by my step-mother, my father having once more entered the state of matrimony with a widow much younger than himself, who had been brought up in a superior manner and was an amiable and sensible woman.

About a year after I had commenced this apprenticeship, my father, finding that he could carry on his business to more advantage in Hull, removed thither with his family. An event of no little importance to me as it in a great measure influenced my future destiny. Hull being one of the best ports in England and a place of great trade, my father had there full employment for his numerous workmen, particularly in vessel work. This naturally leading me to an acquaintance with the sailors on board some of the ships, the many remarkable stories they told me of their voyages and adventures, and of the manners and customs of the nations they had seen, excited a strong wish in me to visit foreign countries, which was increased by my reading the voyages of Captain Cook and some other celebrated navigators.

Thus passed the four years that I lived in Hull, where my father was esteemed by all who knew him as a worthy, industrious, and thriving man. At this period a circumstance occurred which afforded me the opportunity I had for some time wished, of gratifying my inclination of going abroad.

Among our principal customers at Hull were the Americans who frequented that port, and from whose conversation my father as well as myself formed the most favourable opinion of that country as affording an excellent field for the exertions of industry, and a flattering prospect for the establishment of a young man in life. In the summer of the year 1802, during the peace between England and France, the ship *Boston*, belonging to Boston in Massachusetts and commanded by Captain John Salter, arrived at Hull whither she came to take on board a cargo of such goods as were wanted for the trade with the Indians on the Northwest Coast of America. Whence, after having taken in a lading of furs and skins, she was to proceed to China and from thence home to America. The ship having occasion for many repairs and alterations necessary for so long a voyage, the captain applied to my father to do the smith work, which was very considerable. That gentleman, who was of a social turn, used often to call at my father's house, where he passed many of his evenings with his chief and second mates, Mr. B. Debuisa and Mr. William Ingraham, the latter a fine young man of about twenty, of a most amiable temper and of such affable manners as gained him the love and attachment of our whole crew. These gentlemen used occasionally to take me with them to the theatre, an amusement which I was very fond of and which my father rather encouraged than objected to. He thought it a good means of preventing young men, who are naturally inclined to seek for something to amuse them, from frequenting taverns, ale houses, and places of bad resort, equally destructive of the health and morals, while the stage frequently furnished excellent lessons of morality and good conduct.

In the evenings that he passed at my father's, Captain Salter, who had for a great number of years been at sea and seen almost all parts of the world, used sometimes to speak of his voyages. Observing me listen with much attention to his relations, he one day when I had brought him some work said to me in rather a jocose manner, "John, how should you like to go with me?"

I answered that it would give me great pleasure, that I had for a long time wished to visit foreign countries, particularly America, which I had been told so many fine stories of. If my father would give his consent and he was willing to take me with him, I would go.

"I shall be very glad to do it," said he, "if your father can be prevailed on to let you go. I want an expert smith for an armourer, the one I have shipped for that purpose not being sufficiently master of his trade. I have no doubt that you will answer my turn well as I perceive you are both active and ingenious; and on my return to America, I shall probably be able to do something much better for you in Boston. I will take the first opportunity of speaking to your father about it, and try to persuade him to consent."

He accordingly, the next evening that he called at our house, introduced the subject. My father at first would not listen to the proposal. That best of parents, though anxious for my advantageous establishment in life, could not bear to think of parting with me. But on Captain Salter's telling him of what benefit it would be to me to go on the voyage with him, and that it was a pity to keep a promising and ingenious young fellow like myself confined to a small shop in England when, if I had tolerable success, I might do so much better in America where wages were much higher and living cheaper, he at length gave up his objections. He consented that I should ship on board the *Boston* as an armourer at the rate of 30 dollars per month, with an agreement that the amount due me, together with a certain sum of money which my father gave Captain Salter for that purpose, should be laid out by him on the Northwest Coast in the purchase of furs on my account, to be disposed of in China for such goods as would yield a profit on the return of the ship— my father being solicitous to give me every advantage in his power, of well establishing myself in my trade in Boston or some other maritime town of America. Such were the flattering expectations which this good man indulged respecting me. Alas! The fatal disaster that befell us not only blasted all these hopes but involved me in extreme distress and wretchedness for a long period after.

two

Joining the Sailing Ship *Boston*

The ship, having undergone a thorough repair and been well coppered, proceeded to take on board her cargo, which consisted of English cloths, Dutch blankets, looking glasses, beads, knives, razors, &c., which were received from Holland, some sugar and molasses, about 20 hogsheads of rum, including stores for the ship, a great quantity of ammunition, cutlasses, pistols, and 3000 muskets and fowling pieces.

The ship being loaded and ready for sea, as I was preparing for my departure my father came to me, and taking me aside, said to me with much emotion: "John, I am now going to part with you, and heaven only knows if we shall ever again meet. But in whatever part of the world you are, always bear it in mind that on your own conduct will depend your success in life. Be honest, industrious, frugal, and temperate, and you will not fail, in whatsoever country it may be your lot to be placed, to gain yourself friends. Let the Bible be your guide and your reliance in any fortune that may befall you, that Almighty Being, who knows how to bring forth good from evil and who never deserts those who put their trust in him."

He repeated his exhortations to me to lead an honest and a Christian life, and to recollect that I had a father, a mother, a brother, and sister who could not but feel a strong interest in my welfare, enjoining me to write him by the first opportunity that should offer to England, from whatever part of the world I might be in, more particularly on my arrival in Boston. This I promised to do, but long unhappily was it before I was able to fulfill this promise.

I then took an affectionate leave of my worthy parent, whose feelings would hardly permit him to speak, and bidding an affectionate farewell to my brother, sister, and step-mother, who expressed the greatest solicitude for my future fortune, went on board the ship, which proceeded to the Downs to be ready for the first favourable wind. I found myself well accommodated on board as regarded my work, an iron forge having been erected on deck—this my father had made for the ship on a new plan, for which he afterwards obtained a patent—while a corner of the steerage was appropriated to my vice-bench so that in bad weather I could work below.

On the third day of September 1802, we sailed from the Downs with a fair wind, in company with 24 sail of American vessels, most of which were bound home.

I was seasick for a few of the first days, but it was of short continuance. On my recovery I found myself in uncommonly fine health and spirits, and went to work with alacrity at my forge in putting in order some of the muskets and making daggers, knives, and small hatchets for the Indian trade. In wet and stormy weather I was occupied below in filing and polishing them. This was my employment, having but little to do with sailing the vessel, though I used occasionally to lend a hand in assisting the seamen in taking in and making sail.

As I had never before been out of sight of land, I cannot describe my sensations, after I had recovered from the distressing effects of seasickness, on viewing the mightly ocean by which I was surrounded, bounded only by the sky, while its waves rising in mountains seemed every moment to threaten our ruin. Manifest as is the hand of Providence in preserving its creatures from destruction, in no instance is it more so than on the great deep. Whether we consider in its tumultuary motions the watery deluge that each moment menaces to overwhelm us, the immense violence of its shocks, the little that interposes between us and death—a single plank forming our only security, which, should it unfortunately be loosened, would plunge us at once into the abyss—our gratitude ought strongly to be excited towards that superintending Deity who in so wonderful a manner sustains our lives amid the waves.

We had a pleasant and favourable passage of 29 days to the Island of St. Catharine on the coast of Brazil, where the Captain had determined to stop for a few days to wood and water. This place belongs to the Portuguese. On entering the harbour we were saluted by the fort, which we returned. The next day the Governor of the Island came on board of us with his suite. Captain Salter received him with much respect and invited him to dine with him, which he accepted.

The ship remained at St. Catharine four days, during which time we were busily employed in taking in wood, water, and fresh provisions, Captain Salter thinking it best to furnish himself here with a full supply for his voyage to the Northwest Coast so as not to be obliged to stop at the Sandwich Islands [Hawaii]. St. Catharine is a very commodious place for vessels that are bound round Cape Horn to stop at. It abounds with springs of fine water, with excellent oranges, plantains, and bananas.

Having completed our stores we put to sea, and on the 25th of December at length passed Cape Horn, which we had made no less than 36 days before, but were repeatedly forced back by contrary winds, experiencing very rough and tempestuous weather in doubling it.

The *Boston* before it was attacked, as shown in Jewitt's *Narrative*.

Immediately after passing Cape Horn, all our dangers and difficulties seemed to be at an end. The weather became fine, and so little labour was necessary on board the ship that the men soon recovered from their fatigue and were in excellent spirits. A few days after, we fell in with an English South Sea whaling ship, homeward bound, which was the only vessel we spoke with on our voyage. We now took the trade wind, or monsoon, during which we enjoyed the finest weather possible. For the space of a fortnight we were not obliged to reeve a topsail or to make a tack, and so light was the duty and easy the life of the sailors during this time that they appeared the happiest of any people in the world.

Captain Salter, who had been for many years in the East-India trade, was a most excellent seaman and preserved the strictest order and discipline on board his ship, though he was a man of mild temper and conciliating manners and disposed to allow every indulgence to his men not inconsistent with their duty. We had on board a fine band of music with which on Saturday nights, when the weather was pleasant, we were accustomed to be regaled, the Captain ordering them to play for several hours for the amusement of the crew. This to me was most delightful, especially during the serene evenings we experienced in traversing the Southern Ocean. As for myself, during the day I was constantly occupied at my forge in refitting or repairing some of the iron work of the vessel, but principally in making tomahawks, daggers, &c., for the Northwest Coast.

During the first part of our voyage we saw scarcely any fish, excepting some whales, a few sharks, and flying fish. But after weathering Cape Horn we met with numerous shoals of sea porpoises, several of whom we caught. As we had been for some time without fresh provisions, I found it not only a palatable but really a very excellent food. To one who has never before seen them, a shoal of these fish presents a very striking and singular appearance. Beheld at a distance coming towards a vessel, they look not unlike a great number of small black waves rolling over one another in a confused manner and approaching with great swiftness.

As soon as a shoal is seen, all is bustle and activity on board the ship. The grains [an iron instrument with four or more barbed points and an attached line] and the harpoons are immediately got ready, and those who are best skilled in throwing them take their stand at the bow and along the gunwale, anxiously awaiting the welcome troop as they come gambolling and blowing around the vessel in search of food. When pierced with the harpoon and drawn on board, unless the fish is instantly killed by the stroke, which rarely happens, it utters most pitiful cries, greatly resembling those of an infant. The flesh, cut into steaks and broiled, is not unlike very coarse beef, and the harslet [heart, liver, and other internal organs] in appearance and taste is so much like that of a hog that it would be no easy matter to distinguish the one from the other. From this circumstance the sailors have given the name of the herring hog to this fish.

I was told by some of the crew that if one of them happens to free itself from the grains or harpoons when struck, all the others, attracted by the blood, immediately quit the ship and give chase to the wounded one, and as soon as they overtake it, immediately tear it in pieces. We also caught a large shark, which had followed the ship for several days, with a hook that I made for the purpose.

The flesh was by no means equal to that of the herring hog, yet to those destitute as we were of anything fresh, I found it eat very well.

After passing the Cape, when the sea had become calm, we saw great numbers of Albatrosses, a large brown-and-white bird of the goose kind, one of which Captain Salter shot, whose wings measured from their extremities fifteen feet. One thing, however, I must not omit mentioning as it struck me in a most singular and extraordinary manner. This was that on passing Cape Horn in December, which was midsummer in that climate, the nights were so light, without any moon, that we found no difficulty whatever in reading small print, which we frequently did during our watches.

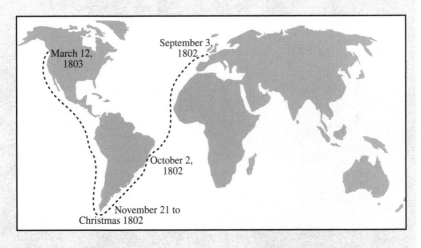

The *Boston* took 78 days to reach the foreboding waters near the tip of South America. After more than a month fighting treacherous conditions, Captain Salter overcame the Cape and took another 75 days to reach Nootka.

three

Nootka Sound

I n this manner, with a fair wind and easy weather from the 28th of December, the period of our passing Cape Horn, we pursued our voyage to the northward until the 12th of March 1803, when we made Woody Point in Nootka Sound on the Northwest Coast of America. We immediately stood up the Sound for Nootka, where Captain Salter had determined to stop in order to supply the ship with wood and water before proceeding up the coast to trade. But in order to avoid the risk of any molestation or interruption to his men from the Indians while thus employed, he proceeded with the ship about five miles to the northward of the village, which is situated on Friendly Cove, and sent out his chief mate with several of the crew in the boat to find a good place for anchoring her.

After sounding for some time, they returned with information that they had discovered a secure place for anchorage on the western side of an inlet or small bay at about half a mile from the coast, near a small island which protected it from the sea, and where there was plenty of wood and excellent water. The ship accordingly came to anchor in this place at twelve o'clock at night, in twelve fathom water, muddy bottom, and so near the shore that to prevent the ship from winding we secured her by a hauser to the trees.

On the morning of the next day, the 13th, several of the natives came on board in a canoe from the village of Nootka with their king, called Maquinna, who appeared much pleased on seeing us and, with great seeming cordiality, welcomed Captain Salter and his

The *Boston* was greeted by Maquinna and members of the tribe in dugout canoes. These grand canoes were common on the Northwest Coast because of the availability of the giant red cedar.

officers to his country. As I had never before beheld a savage of any nation, it may readily be supposed that the novelty of their appearance, so different from any people that I had hitherto seen, excited in me strong feelings of surprise and curiosity. I was, however, particularly struck with the looks of their king, who was a man of a dignified aspect, about six feet in height and extremely strait and well proportioned.

A rendition of Boston Cove in Nootka Sound, where tragedy struck the *Boston*.

His features were in general good, and his face was rendered remarkable by a large Roman nose, a very uncommon form of feature among these people. His complexion was of a dark copper hue, though his face, legs, and arms were on this occasion so covered with red paint that their natural colour could scarcely be perceived. His eyebrows were painted black in two broad stripes like a new moon, and his long black hair, which shone with oil, was fastened in a bunch on the top of his head and strewed or powdered all over with white down [the soft underplumage of birds], which gave him a most curious and extraordinary appearance.

He was dressed in a large mantle or cloak of the black sea otter skin, which reached to his knees and was fastened around his middle by a broad belt of the cloth of the country [woven or shredded cedar bark] wrought, or painted, with figures of several colours. This dress was by no means unbecoming, but on the contrary had an air of savage magnificence. His men were habited in mantles of the same cloth, which is made from the bark of a tree and has some resemblance to straw matting. These are nearly square and have two holes in the upper part large enough to admit the arms. They reach as low as the knees and are fastened around their bodies with a belt about four inches broad of the same cloth.

From his having frequently visited the English and American ships that traded to the coast, Maquinna had learned the signification of a number of English words and in general could make himself pretty well understood by us in our own language. He was always the first to go on board such ships as came to Nootka, which he was much pleased in visiting, even when he had no trade to offer, as he almost always received some small present and was in general extremely well treated by the commanders. He remained on board of us for some time, during which the Captain took him into the cabin and treated him with a glass of rum—these people being very fond of distilled spirits— and some biscuit and molasses, which they prefer to any kind of food that we can offer them.

A sketch of some members of the Mowachaht tribe by Cook's sketch artist, John Webber. The Nuu-chah-nulth followed policies of primogeniture, and an ideal *Tyee* (chief) was the eldest son of an eldest son as far back as possible.

As there are seldom many furs to be purchased at this place, and it was not fully the season, Captain Salter had put in here not so much with an expectation of trading as to procure an ample stock of wood and water for the supply of the ship on the coast, thinking it more prudent to take it on board at Nootka, from the generally friendly disposition of the people, than to endanger the safety of his men in sending them on shore for that purpose among the more ferocious natives of the north. With this view, we immediately set about getting our water casks in readiness.

The next and two succeeding days, part of the crew were sent on shore to cut pine timber and assist the carpenter in making it into yards and spars for the ship, while those on board were employed in refitting the rigging, repairing the sails, &c., when we proceeded to take in our wood and water as expeditiously as possible, during which time I kept myself busily employed in repairing the muskets, making knives, tomaxes [possibly a hatchet or tomahawk], &c., and doing such iron work as was wanted for the ship.

Meanwhile, more or less of the natives came on board of us daily, bringing with them fresh salmon with which they supplied us in great plenty, receiving in return some trifling articles. Captain Salter was always very particular, before admitting these people on board, to see that they had no arms about them by obliging them indiscriminately to throw off their garments, so that he felt perfectly secure from any attack.

On the 15th the king came on board with several of his chiefs. He was dressed as before in his magnificent otter skin robe, having his face highly painted, and his hair tossed off with the white down which looked like snow. His chiefs were dressed in mantles of the country cloth of its natural colour, which is a pale yellow. These were ornamented with a broad border painted or wrought in figures of several colours representing men's heads, various animals, &c., and secured around them by a belt like that of the king, from which it was distinguished only by being narrower. The dress of the common people is of the same fashion and differs from that of the chiefs in being of a coarser texture and painted red, of one uniform colour.

Captain Salter invited Maquinna and his chiefs to dine with him, and it was curious to see how these people seat themselves with their feet under them crossed like Turks. They cannot endure the taste of salt, and the only thing they would eat with us was the ship bread, which they were very fond of, especially when dipped in molasses. They had also a great liking for tea and coffee when well sweetened.

As iron weapons and tools of almost every kind are in much request among them, whenever they came on board they were always very attentive to me, crowding around me at the forge as if to see in what manner I did my work, and in this way became quite familiar, a circumstance, as will be seen in the end, of great importance to me.

The salmon which they brought us furnished a most delicious treat to men who for a long time had lived wholly on salt provisions excepting such few sea fish as we had the good fortune occasionally to take. We indeed feasted most luxuriously and flattered ourselves that we should not want while on the coast for plenty of fresh provisions, little imagining the fate that awaited us, and that this dainty food was to prove the unfortunate lure to our destruction!

On the 19th the king came again on board and was invited by the Captain to dine with him. He had much conversation with Captain Salter and informed him that there were plenty of wild ducks and geese near Friendly Cove, on which the Captain made him a present of a double-barrelled fowling piece with which he appeared to be greatly pleased and soon after went on shore.

On the 20th we were nearly ready for our departure, having taken in what wood and water we were in want of.

The next day Maquinna came on board with nine pair of wild ducks as a present. At the same time he brought with him the gun, one of the locks of which he had broken, telling the Captain that it was *peshak;* that is, bad. Captain Salter was very much offended at this observation, and considering it as a mark of contempt for his present, he called the king a liar, adding other opprobrious terms, and taking the gun from him, tossed it indignantly into the cabin. Calling me to him, he said, "John, this fellow has broken this beautiful fowling piece. See if you can mend it."

On examining it I told him that it could be done. As I have already observed, Maquinna knew a number of English words and unfortunately understood but too well the meaning of the reproachful terms that the Captain addressed to him. He said not a word in reply, but his countenance sufficiently expressed the rage he felt, though he exerted himself to suppress it. I observed him, while the Captain was speaking, repeatedly put his hand to his throat and rub it upon his bosom, which he afterwards told me was to keep down his heart which was rising into his throat and choking him. He soon after went on shore with his men, evidently much discomposed.

four

Massacre

On the morning of the 22nd the natives came off to us as usual with salmon and remained on board. About noon, Maquinna came alongside with a considerable number of his chiefs and men in their canoes who, after going through the customary examination, were admitted into the ship. He had a whistle in his hand and over his face a very ugly mask of wood representing the head of some wild beast, appeared to be remarkably good humoured and gay, and whilst his people sung and capered about the deck, entertaining us with a variety of antic tricks and gestures, he blew his whistle to a kind of tune which seemed to regulate their motions. As Captain Salter was walking on the quarter deck, amusing himself with their dancing, the king came up to him and enquired when he intended to go to sea. He answered, "Tomorrow."

Maquinna then said, "You love salmon—much in Friendly Cove, why not go then and catch some?"

The Captain thought that it would be very desirable to have a good supply of these fish for the voyage. On consulting with Mr. Debuisa it was agreed to send part of the crew on shore after dinner with the seine in order to procure a quantity. Maquinna

Maquinna, the most famous chief of the West Coast people. The word *maquinna* actually means "chief" in the Mowachaht language, but was misunderstood to be his personal name by Captain Cook and others.

and his chiefs stayed and dined on board. After dinner the chief mate went off with nine men in the jolly boat and yawl to fish at Friendly Cove, having set the steward on shore at our watering place to wash the captain's clothes. Shortly after the departure of the boats I went down to my vice-bench in the steerage, where I was employed in cleaning muskets.

Masks were essential to ceremonies, and the animals they represented were links to the spirit world.

I had not been there more than an hour when I heard the men hoisting in the long boat, which in a few minutes after was succeeded by a great bustle and confusion on deck. I immediately ran up the steerage stairs, but scarcely was my head above deck when I was caught by the hair by one of the savages and lifted from my feet. Fortunately for me, my hair being short and the ribbon with which it was tied slipping, I fell from his hold into the steerage.

As I was falling he struck at me with an axe, which cut a deep gash in my forehead and penetrated the skull. But in consequence of his losing his hold I luckily escaped the full force of the blow which, otherwise, would have cleft my head in two. I fell stunned and senseless upon the floor. How long I continued in this situation I know not, but on recovering my senses, the first thing that I did was to try to get up. But so weak was I from the loss of blood that I fainted and fell. I was, however, soon recalled to my recollection by three loud shouts or yells from the savages, which convinced me that they had got possession of the ship.

It is impossible for me to describe my feelings at this terrific sound. Some faint idea may be formed by those who have known what it is to half waken from a hideous dream and still think it

real. Never, no, never shall I lose from my mind the impression
of that dreadful moment. I expected every instant to share the
wretched fate of my unfortunate companions, and when I heard
the song of triumph by which these infernal yells was succeeded,
my blood ran cold in my veins. Having at length sufficiently
recovered my senses to look around me after wiping the blood
from my eyes, I saw that the hatch of the steerage was shut.

This was done, as I afterwards discovered, by order of
Maquinna who, on seeing the savage strike at me with the axe,
told him not to hurt me, for I was the armourer and would be
useful to them in repairing their arms; while at the same time, to
prevent any of his men from injuring me, he had the hatch closed.
But to me this circumstance wore a very different appearance. I
thought that these barbarians had only prolonged my life in order
to deprive me of it by the most cruel tortures.

I remained in this horrid state of suspense for a very long
time. At length the hatch was opened and Maquinna, calling me
by name, ordered me to come up. I groped my way up as well as
I was able, being almost blinded with the blood that flowed from
my wound, and so weak I had difficulty walking.

The king, on perceiving my situation, ordered one of his
men to bring a pot of water to wash the blood from my face,
which having done, I was able to see distinctly with one of my
eyes. The other was so swollen from my wounds that it was closed.
But what a terrific spectacle met my eyes. Six naked savages,
standing in a circle around me, covered with the blood of my
murdered comrades, with their daggers uplifted in their hands,
prepared to strike. I now thought my last moment had come and
recommended my soul to my Maker.

The king who, as I have already observed, knew enough
English to make himself understood, entered the circle, and
placing himself before me, addressed me in the following words:
"John—I speak—you no say no—you say no—daggers come!"

He then asked me if I would be his slave during my life, if I
would fight for him in his battles, if I would repair his muskets
and make daggers and knives for him—with several other
questions, to all of which I was careful to answer yes. He then

told me that he would spare my life and ordered me to kiss his hands and feet to show my submission to him, which I did. In the meantime his people were very clamorous to have me put to death so that there should be none of us left to tell our story to our countrymen and prevent them from coming to trade with them. But the king, in the most determined manner, opposed their wishes, and to his favour am I wholly indebted for my being yet among the living.

As I was busy at work at the time of the attack, I was without my coat. What with the coldness of the weather, my feebleness from loss of blood, the pain of my wound, and the extreme agitation and terror that I still felt, I shook like a leaf, which the king observing, went into the cabin. Bringing up a great coat that belonged to the Captain, he threw it over my shoulders, telling me to drink some rum from a bottle which he handed me at the same time, giving me to understand that it would be good for me and keep me from trembling as I did.

I took a draught of it, after which, taking me by the hand, he led me to the quarter deck, where the most horrid sight presented itself that ever my eyes witnessed—the heads of our unfortunate Captain and his crew, to the number of 25, were all arranged in a line. Maquinna, ordering one of his people to bring a head, asked me whose it was. I answered, the Captain's.

In like manner the others were showed to me. I told him the names, excepting a few that were so horribly mangled that I was not able to recognize them. I now discovered that all our unfortunate crew had been massacred. After getting possession of the ship, the savages had broke open the arm chest and magazine, and supplying themselves with ammunition and arms, sent a party on shore to attack our men who had gone thither to fish, and being joined by numbers from the village, without difficulty overpowered and murdered them, and cutting off their heads, brought them on board, after throwing their bodies into the sea.

On looking upon the deck I saw it entirely covered with the blood of my poor comrades, whose throats had been cut with their own jack-knives, the savages having seized the opportunity

Names of the Crew of the Ship Boston, belonging to
Boston in Massachusetts, owned by Messrs. F. & T.
Amory, Merchants of that place—All of whom excepting
two, were on the 22d of March, 1803, barbarously
murdered by the Savages at Nootka.

John Salter,	of Boston,	Captain.
B. Delouissa,	Do.	Chief-Mate.
William Ingraham,	of New-York,	Second-Mate.
Edward Thompson,	of Blyth, (England,)	Boatswain.
Adam Siddle,	of Hull, Do.	Carpenter.
Philip Brown,	of Cambridge, (Mass.)	Joiner.
John Dorthy,	of Scituate, Do.	Blacksmith.
Abraham Waters,	of Philadelphia,	Steward.
Francis Duffield,	of Penton, (England,)	Tailor.
John Wilson, (blackman)	of Virginia,	Cook.
William Caldwell,	of Boston,	Seaman.
Joseph Miner,	of Newburyport,	Do.
William Robinson,	of Leigh, (Scotland,)	Do.
Thomas Wilson,	of Air, Do.	Do.
Andrew Kelly,	Do. Do.	Do.
Robert Burton,	of the Isle of Man,	Do.
James M'Clay,	of Dublin,	Do.
Thomas Platteh,	of Blakeney, Norfolk, Eng.	Do.
Thomas Newton,	of Hull, Do.	Do.
Charles Bates,	of St. James Deeping, Do.	Do.
John Hall,	of New-Castle, Do.	Do.
Samuel Wood,	of Glasgow, (Scotland,)	Do.
Peter Alstrom,	Norwegian,	Do.
Francis Marten,	Portuguese,	Do.
Jupiter Senegal, (blackman)		Do.
John Thompson,	Philadelphia,	Sail-Maker,

who escaped—since dead.

John R. Jewitt of Boston, in England, Armourer,
the writer of the Journal from whence this Narrative is taken, and who at
present, July, 1815, resides in Middletown, in the State of Connecticut.

A list of the crew of the Boston, as it appeared in Jewitt's *Narrative.*

while they were busy in hoisting in the boat to grapple with them and overpower them by their numbers. In the scuffle the Captain was thrown overboard and despatched by those in the canoes, who immediately cut off his head. What I felt on this occasion may be more readily conceived than expressed.

After I had answered his questions, Maquinna took my silk handkerchief from my neck and bound it around my head, placing over the wound a leaf of tobacco, of which we had a quantity on board. This was done at my desire, as I had often found from personal experience the benefit of this application to cuts.

Maquinna then ordered me to get the ship under weigh for Friendly Cove. This I did by cutting the cables and sending some of the natives aloft to loose the sails, which they performed in a very bungling manner. But they succeeded so far in loosing the jib and topsails that, with the advantage of a fair wind, I succeeded in getting the ship into the Cove. Here, by order of the king, I ran her ashore on a sandy beach at eight o'clock at night.

We were received by the inhabitants of the village, men, women, and children, with loud shouts of joy and a most horrible drumming with sticks upon the roofs and sides of their houses, in which they had also stuck a great number of lighted pine torches to welcome their king's return and congratulate him on the success of his enterprise.

five

Becoming
Maquinna's Slaves

Maquinna then took me on shore to his house, which was very large and filled with people. Here I was received with much kindness by the women, particularly those belonging to the king, who had no less than nine wives, all of whom came around me expressing much sympathy for my misfortune, gently stroking and patting my head in an encouraging and soothing manner with words expressive of condolence. How sweet is compassion, even from savages? Those who have been in a similar situation can alone truly appreciate its value.

In the meantime, all the warriors of the tribe, to the number of 500, had assembled at the king's house to rejoice for their success. They exulted greatly in having taken our ship, and each one boasted of his own particular exploits in killing our men. But they were in general much dissatisfied with my having been suffered to live and were very urgent with Maquinna to deliver me to them to be put to death. He obstinately refused, telling them that he had promised me my life and would not break his word and that besides, I knew how to repair and to make arms and should be of great use to them.

The king then seated me by him and ordered his women to bring him something to eat. They set before him some dried clams and train oil [rendered from the fat, or blubber, of whales], of which he ate very heartily and encouraged me to follow his example, telling me to eat much and take a great deal of oil which would make me strong and fat. Notwithstanding his praise of this new kind of food, I felt no disposition to indulge in it, both the smell and taste being loathsome to me. Had it been otherwise, such was the pain I endured, the agitation of my mind, and the gloominess of my reflections that I should have felt very little inclination for eating.

Not satisfied with his first refusal to deliver me up to them, the people again became clamorous that Maquinna should consent to my being killed, saying that not one of us ought to be left alive to give information to others of our countrymen and prevent them from coming to trade or induce them to revenge the destruction of our ship. They at length became so boisterous that he caught up a large club in a passion and drove them all out of the house. During this scene a son of the king, of about eleven years old, attracted no doubt by the singularity of my appearance, came up to me. I caressed him. He returned my attentions with much apparent pleasure, and, considering this as a fortunate opportunity to gain the good will of the father, I took the child on my knee. Cutting the metal buttons from the coat I had on, I tied them around his neck. At this he was highly delighted and became so much attached to me that he would not quit me.

The king appeared much pleased with my attention to his son, and telling me that it was time to go to sleep, directed me to lie with his son next to him, as he was afraid lest some of his

Maquinna's house at Tahsis, where the tribe went for the winter. The skins in the background contain train oil. When European explorers entered into homes like this, they frequently complained of their relative lack of cleanliness. However, the Mowachaht were avid bathers, unlike their European counterparts. (Drawn by a Spanish artist in 1792.)

people would come while he was asleep and kill me with their daggers. I lay down as he ordered me, but neither the state of my mind nor the pain I felt would allow me to sleep.

About midnight I was greatly alarmed by the approach of one of the natives, who came to give information to the king that there was one of the white men alive, who had knocked him down as he went on board the ship at night. This Maquinna communicated to me, giving me to understand that as soon as the sun rose he should kill him. I endeavoured to persuade him to spare his life, but he bade me be silent and go to sleep.

I said nothing more but lay revolving in my mind what method I could devise to save the life of this man. What a consolation, thought I, what a happiness would it prove to me in my forlorn state among these heathen, to have a Christian and one of my own countrymen for a companion, and how greatly would it alleviate and lighten the burden of my slavery.

As I was thinking of some plan for his preservation, it all at once came into my mind that this man was probably the sail-maker of the ship, named Thompson. I had not seen his head among those on deck and knew that he was below at work upon the sails not long before the attack. The more I thought of it, the more probable it appeared to me. As Thompson was a man nearly 40 years of age and had an old look, I conceived it would be easy to make him pass for my father, and by this means prevail on Maquinna to spare his life. Towards morning I fell into a doze, but was awakened with the first beams of the sun by the king, who told me that he was going to kill the man who was on board the ship and ordered me to accompany him. I rose and followed him, leading with me the young prince, his son.

On coming to the beach I found all the men of the tribe assembled. The king addressed them, saying that one of the white men had been found alive on board the ship, and requested their opinion as to saving his life or putting him to death. They were unanimously for death. This determination he made known to me. Having arranged my plan, I asked him, pointing to the boy whom I still held by the hand, if he loved his son. He answered that he did. I then asked the child if he loved his father, and on replying in the affirmative, I said, "And I also love mine."

I then threw myself on my knees at Maquinna's feet and implored him with tears in my eyes to spare my father's life, if the man on board should prove to be him, telling him that if he killed my father it was my wish that he should kill me too, and that if he did not I would kill myself, and that he would thus lose my services. Whereas, by sparing my father's life he would preserve mine, which would be of great advantage to him by my repairing and making arms for him.

Maquinna appeared moved by my entreaties and promised not to put the man to death if he should be my father. He then explained to his people what I had said and ordered me to go on board and tell the man to come to shore.

To my unspeakable joy on going into the hold I found that my conjecture was true. Thompson was there. He had escaped without any injury excepting a slight wound in the nose, given

him by one of the savages with a knife as he attempted to come
on deck during the scuffle. Finding the savages in possession
of the ship, as he afterwards informed me, he secreted himself
in the hold, hoping for some chance to make his escape, but
that the Indian who came on board in the night approaching the
place where he was, he supposed himself discovered. Being
determined to sell his life as dearly as possible, as soon as he
came within his reach he knocked him down, but the Indian
immediately springing up, ran off at full speed.

I informed him in a few words that all our men had been
killed, that the king had preserved my life, and had consented
to spare his on the supposition that he was my father, an opinion
which he must be careful not to undeceive them in as it was his
only safety. After giving him his cue, I went on shore with him
and presented him to Maquinna, who immediately knew him to
be the sailmaker and was much pleased, observing that he could
make sails for his canoe. He then took us to his house and ordered
something for us to eat.

On the 24th and 25th the natives were busily employed in
taking the cargo out of the ship, stripping her of her sails and
rigging, cutting away the spars and masts, and in short rendering
her as complete a wreck as possible, the muskets, ammunition,
cloth, and all the principal articles taken from her being deposited
in the king's house.

While they were thus occupied, each one taking what he
liked, my companion and myself being obliged to aid them, I
thought it best to secure the accounts and papers of the ship in
hopes that on some future day I might have it in my power to
restore them to the owners.

With this view I took possession of the Captain's writing desk,
which contained the most of them, together with some paper and
implements of writing. I had also the good fortune to find a blank
account book in which I resolved, should it be permitted me, to
write an account of our capture and the most remarkable
occurrences that I should meet with during my stay among these
people, fondly indulging the hope that it would not be long before
some vessel would arrive to release us. I likewise found in the

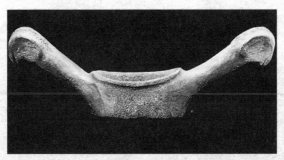

A ceremonial cup made from antlers (above) and a ceremonial axe (page 50). Songs were integral parts of ceremonies, and as songs were the property of individuals, it was improper to sing someone else's song without permission.

cabin a small volume of sermons, a Bible, and a common prayer book of the Church of England. They furnished me and my comrade great consolation in the midst of our mournful servitude and enabled me, under the favour of divine providence, to support with firmness the miseries of a life which I might otherwise have found beyond my strength to endure.

As these people set no value upon things of this kind, I found no difficulty in appropriating them to myself by putting them in my chest, which though it had been broken open and rifled by the savages, I still had the key and without much difficulty secured it. In this I also put some small tools belonging to the ship, with several other articles, particularly a journal kept by the second mate, Mr. Ingraham, and a collection of drawings and views of places taken by him, which I had the good fortune to preserve. On my arrival at Boston I gave them to a connection of his, the Honourable Judge Dawes, who sent them to his family in New York.

On the 26th, two ships were seen standing in for Friendly Cove. At their first appearance the inhabitants were thrown into great confusion, but soon collecting a number of muskets and blunderbusses, ran to the shore, from whence they kept up so brisk a fire at them that they were evidently afraid to approach nearer. After firing a few rounds of grapeshot, which did no harm to anyone, they wore ship and stood out to sea. These ships, as I afterwards learned, were the *Mary* and *Juno* of Boston.

They were scarcely out of sight when Maquinna expressed much regret that he had permitted his people to fire at them, being apprehensive that they would give information to others in what manner they had been received, and prevent them from coming to trade with him.

A few days after hearing of the capture of the ship, there arrived at Nootka a great number of canoes filled with savages from no less than twenty tribes to the north and south. Among those from the north were the Ai-tiz-

A ceremonial axe of the Mowachaht.

zarts, Schoo-mad-its, Neu-wit-ties, Savin-nars, Ah-owz-arts, Mo-watch-its, Suth-setts, Neu-chad-lits, Mich-la-its and Cay-u-quets; the most of whom were considered as tributary to Nootka. From the south, the A-y-charts and Hesquiahts also tributary, with the Kla-oo-quates, and the Wickanninish, a large and powerful tribe about 200 miles distant. These last were better clad than most of the others, and their canoes wrought with much greater skill. They are furnished with sails as well as paddles, and with the advantage of a fair breeze, are usually but 24 hours on their passage.

Maquinna, who was very proud of his new acquisition, was desirous of welcoming these visitors in the European manner. He accordingly ordered his men, as the canoes approached, to assemble on the beach with loaded muskets and blunderbusses, placing Thompson at the cannon, which had been brought from the ship and laid upon two long sticks of timber in front of the village. Then taking a speaking trumpet in his hand, he ascended with me the roof of his house and began drumming or beating upon the boards with a stick most violently.

Nothing could be more ludicrous than the appearance of this motley group of savages collected on the shore, dressed as they were with their ill-gotten finery in the most fantastic manner. Some were in women's smocks, taken from our cargo, others in *kutsacks* (or cloaks) of blue, red, or yellow broadcloth, with stockings drawn over their heads, and their necks hung round with numbers of powder horns, shot bags, and cartouche boxes, some of them having no less than ten muskets apiece on their shoulders, and five or six daggers in their girdles. Diverting indeed was it to see them all squatted upon the beach, holding their muskets perpendicularly with the butt pressed upon the sand instead of against their shoulders, and in this position awaited the order to fire. Maquinna, at last, called to them with his trumpet to fire, which they did in the most awkward and timid manner, with their muskets hard pressed upon the ground as mentioned.

At the same moment the cannon was fired by Thompson, they threw themselves back and began to roll and tumble over the sand as if they had been shot. Suddenly springing up, they began a song of triumph, and running backward and forward upon the shore with the wildest gesticulations, boasted of their exploits and exhibited as trophies what they had taken from us. Notwithstanding the unpleasantness of my situation and the feelings that this display of our spoils excited, I could not avoid laughing at the strange appearance of these savages, their awkward movements, and the singular contrast of their dress and arms.

When the ceremony was concluded, Maquinna invited the strangers to a feast at his house consisting of whale blubber, smoked herring spawn, and dried fish and train oil, of which they eat most plentifully. The feast being over, the trays out of which they eat and other things were immediately removed to make room for the dance which was to close the entertainment. This was performed by Maquinna's son, the young prince Satsat-sok-sis, whom I have already spoken of, in the following manner: Three of the principal chiefs, dressed in their otter skin mantles, which they wore only on extraordinary occasions and at festivals, having their heads covered over with white down, and their faces highly painted, came forward into the middle of the room, each furnished with a bag filled with the white down, which they scattered around in such a manner as to represent a fall of snow. These were followed by the young prince, who was dressed in a long piece of yellow cloth wrapped loosely around him, and decorated with small bells, with a cap on his head to which was fastened a curious mask in imitation of a wolf's head. The rear was brought up by the king himself in his robe of sea otter skin, with a small whistle in his mouth and a rattle in his hand, with which he kept time to a sort of tune on his whistle.

After passing very rapidly in this order around the house, each of them seated himself, except the prince, who immediately began his dance, which principally consisted in springing up into the air in a squat posture and constantly turning around on his heels with great swiftness in a very narrow circle. This dance, with a few intervals of rest, was continued for about two hours, during which the chiefs kept up a constant drumming with sticks of about a foot in length on a long hollow plank which was, though very noisy, a most doleful kind of music. This they accompanied with songs, the king himself acting as chorister, while the women applauded each feat of activity in the dancer by repeating the words *Wocash! Wocash Tyee!* That is good! Very good prince!

As soon as the dance was finished, Maquinna began to give presents to the strangers in the name of his son Sat-sat-sok-sis. These were pieces of European cloth generally of a fathom in length, muskets, powder, shot, &c. Whenever he gave them anything, they had a peculiar manner of snatching it from him with a very stern and surly look, repeating each time the words *Wocash Tyee.* This I understood to be their custom and was considered as a compliment, which if omitted would be supposed as a mark of disregard for the present. On this occasion Maquinna gave away no less than 100 muskets, the same number of looking glasses, 400 yards of cloth, and 20 casks of powder, besides other things.

After receiving these presents, the strangers retired on board their canoes, for so numerous were they that Maquinna would not suffer any but the chiefs to sleep in the houses. In order to prevent the property from being pillaged by them, he ordered Thompson and myself to keep guard during the night, armed with cutlasses and pistols.

In this manner tribes of savages from various parts of the coast continued coming for several days, bringing with them blubber, oil, herring spawn, dried fish, and clams, for which they received in return presents of cloth, &c., after which they in general immediately returned home. I observed that very few, if any of them, except the chiefs, had arms, which I afterwards learned is the custom with these people whenever they come upon a friendly visit or to trade, in order to show on their approach that their intentions are pacific.

six

A Fire Destroys the *Boston*

E arly on the morning of the 18th, the ship was discovered
to be on fire. This was owing to one of the savages having
gone on board with a firebrand at night for the purpose of
plunder, some sparks from which fell into the hold and,
communicating with some combustibles, soon enveloped the
whole in flames. The natives regretted the loss of the ship, the
more as a great part of her cargo still remained on board. To my
companion and myself it was a most melancholy sight, for with
her disappeared from our eyes every trace of a civilized country.
But the disappointment we experienced was still more severely
felt, for we had calculated on having the provision to ourselves,
which would have furnished us with a stock for years, as whatever
is cured with salt, together with most of our other articles of
food, are never eaten by these people.

I had luckily saved all my tools excepting the anvil and the bellows, which was attached to the forge and because of their great weight had not been brought on shore. We had also the good fortune, in looking over what had been taken from the ship, to discover a box of chocolate and a case of port wine, which as the Indians were not fond of it, proved a great comfort to us for some time. From one of the natives I obtained a nautical almanac, which had belonged to the Captain, and which was of great use to me in determining the time.

About two days after, on examining their booty, the savages found a tierce [a cask which held some 42 gallons] of rum with which they were highly delighted, as they have become very fond of spirituous liquors since their intercourse with the whites. This was towards evening, and Maquinna having assembled all the men at his house, gave a feast at which they drank so freely of the rum that in a short time they became so extremely wild and frantic that Thompson and myself, apprehensive for our safety, thought it prudent to retire privately into the woods where we continued till past midnight.

On our return we found the women gone, who are always very temperate, drinking nothing but water, having quitted the house and gone to the other huts to sleep, so terrified were they at the conduct of the men, who all lay stretched out on the floor in a state of complete intoxication. How easy in this situation would it have been for us to have dispatched or made ourselves masters of our enemies had there been any ship near to which we could have escaped. But as we were situated, the attempt would have been madness.

The wish of revenge was, however, less strongly impressed on my mind than what appeared to be so evident an interposition of divine Providence in our favour. How little can man penetrate its designs, and how frequently is that intended as a blessing which he views as a curse. The burning of our ship, which we had lamented so much as depriving us of so many comforts, now appeared to us in a very different light. For had the savages got possession of the rum, of which there were nearly twenty puncheons [a puncheon was a cask that usually held 80 gallons] on board, we must inevitably have fallen a sacrifice to their fury in some of their moments of intoxication. This cask, fortunately, and a case of gin was all the spirits they obtained from the ship. To prevent the recurrence of similar danger I examined the cask, and finding still a considerable quantity remaining, I bored a small hole in the bottom with a gimblet, which before morning to my great joy completely emptied it.

By this time the wound in my head began to be much better, so that I could enjoy some sleep, which I had been almost deprived of by the pain. Though I was still feeble from the loss of blood and my sufferings, I found myself sufficiently well to go to work at my trade in making for the king and his wives bracelets and other small ornaments of copper or steel, and in repairing the arms, making use of a large square stone for the anvil, and heating my metal in a common wood fire. This was very gratifying to Maquinna and his women particularly, and secured me their good will.

In the meantime, great numbers from the other tribes kept continually flocking to Nootka, bringing with them in exchange for the ship's plunder such quantities of provision that, notwithstanding the little success that Maquinna met with in whaling this season and their gluttonous waste, always eating to excess when they have it, regardless of the morrow, seldom did the natives experience any want of food during the summer.

As to myself and companion, we fared as they did, never wanting for such provision as they had, though we were obliged to eat it cooked in their manner and with train oil as a sauce, a circumstance not a little unpleasant, both from their uncleanly mode of cooking, and many of the articles of their food which to a European are very disgusting. But, as the saying is, hunger will break through stone walls, and we found at times in the blubber of sea animals and the flesh of the dog fish, loathsome as it in general was, a very acceptable repast.

But much oftener would poor Thompson, who was no favourite with them, have suffered from hunger had it not been for my furnishing him with provision. This I was enabled to do from my work, Maquinna allowing me the privilege, when not employed for him, to work for myself in making bracelets and other ornaments of copper, fish-hooks, daggers, &c., either to sell to the tribes who visited us, or for our own chiefs. On these occasions, besides supplying me with as much as I wished to eat and a sufficiency for Thompson, they almost always made me a present of a European garment taken from the ship or some fathoms of cloth, which were made up by my comrade and enabled us to go comfortably clad for some time, or small bundles of penknives, razors, scissors, &c., for one of which we could almost always procure from the natives two or three fresh salmon, cod, or halibut, or dried fish, clams, and herring spawn from the stranger tribes. Had we only been permitted to cook them after our own way, as we had pots and other utensils belonging to the ship, we should not have had much cause of complaint in this respect.

But so tenacious are these people of their customs, particularly in the article of food and cooking, that the king always obliged me to give whatever provisions I bought to the women to cook. One day, finding Thompson and myself on the shore employed in boiling down sea water into salt, on being told what it was he was very much displeased, and taking the little we had procured, threw it into the sea. In one instance alone, as a particular favour, he allowed me to boil some salmon in my own way. When I invited him and his queen to eat with me they tasted it, but did not like it and made their meal of some of it that I had cooked in their country fashion.

In May, the weather became uncommonly mild and pleasant, and so forward was vegetation that I picked a plenty of strawberries by the middle of the month. Of this fruit there are great quantities on this coast, and I found them a most delicious treat. My health had now become almost re-established, my wound being so far healed that it gave me no farther trouble. I had never failed to wash it regularly once a day in sea water, and to dress it with a fresh leaf of tobacco which I obtained from the natives, who had taken it from the ship but made no use of it. This was all the dressing I gave it, except applying to it two or three times a little loaf sugar, which Maquinna gave me, in order to remove some proud flesh [tissue formed when a wound begins to heal] which prevented it from closing.

My cure would doubtless have been much sooner effected had I have been in a civilized country where I could have had it dressed by a surgeon and properly attended to. But alas! I had no good Samaritan with oil and wine to bind up my wounds, and fortunate might I even esteem myself that I was permitted to dress it myself. The utmost that I could expect from the natives was compassion for my misfortune, which I indeed experienced from the women, particularly the queen, or favourite wife of Maquinna, the mother of Sat-sat-sok-sis, who used frequently to point to my head and manifest much kindness and solicitude for me. I must do Maquinna the justice to acknowledge that he always appeared desirous of sparing me any labour which he believed might be hurtful to me, frequently enquiring in an affectionate manner if my head pained me. As for the others, some of the chiefs excepted, they cared little what became of me and probably would have been gratified with my death.

My health being at length re-established and my wound healed, Thompson became anxious for me to begin my journal. As I had no ink, he proposed to cut his finger to supply me with blood for the purpose whenever I should want it. On the first of June I accordingly commenced a regular diary, but had no occasion to make use of the expedient suggested by my comrade, having found a much better substitute in the expressed juice of a certain plant which furnished me with a bright green colour.

After making a number of trials I at length succeeded in obtaining a very tolerable ink by boiling the juice of the blackberry with a mixture of finely powdered charcoal and filtering it through a cloth. This I afterwards preserved in bottles and found it answer very well, so true is it that "necessity is the mother of invention." As for quills, I found no difficulty in procuring them, whenever I wanted, from the crows and ravens with which the beach was almost always covered, attracted by the offal of whales, seals, &c., and which were so tame that I could easily kill them with stones, while a large clam shell furnished me with an ink stand.

The extreme solicitude of Thompson that I should begin my journal might be considered as singular in a man who neither knew how to write or read, a circumstance, by the way, very uncommon in an American, he having been for many years at sea, and accustomed to consider the keeping of a journal as a thing indispensable. This man was born in Philadelphia, and at eight years old ran away from his friends and entered as a cabin boy on board a ship bound to London. On his arrival there, finding himself in distress, he engaged as an apprentice to the captain of a collier, from whence he was impressed on board an English man of war. He continued in the British naval service about 27 years, during which he was present at the engagement under Lord Howe with the French fleet in June 1794, and when peace was made between England and France, was discharged. He was a very strong and powerful man, an expert boxer, and perfectly fearless. Indeed, so little was his dread of danger that when irritated he was wholly regardless of his life.

One evening about the middle of April, as I was at the house of one of the chiefs where I had been employed on some work for him, word was brought me that Maquinna was going to kill Thompson. I immediately hurried home, where I found the king in the act of presenting a loaded musket at Thompson, who was standing before him with his breast bared and calling on him to fire. I instantly stepped up to Maquinna, who was foaming with rage. Addressing him in soothing words, I begged him for my sake not to kill my father, and at length succeeded in taking the musket from him and persuading him to sit down.

On enquiring into the cause of his anger, I learned that while Thompson was lighting the lamps in the king's room, Maquinna having substituted ours for their pine torches, some of the boys began to tease him, running around him and pulling him by the trousers, among the most forward of whom was the young prince. This caused Thompson to spill the oil, which threw him into such a passion that, without caring what he did, he struck the prince so violent a blow in his face with his fist as to knock him down. The sensation excited among the savages by an act which was considered as the highest indignity and a profanation of the sacred person of majesty may be easily conceived.

The king was immediately acquainted with it, who, on coming in and seeing his son's face covered with blood, seized a musket and began to load it, determined to take instant revenge on the audacious offender. Had I arrived a few minutes later than I did, my companion would certainly have paid with his life for his rash and violent conduct. I found the utmost difficulty in pacifying Maquinna, who for a long time after could not forgive Thompson, but would repeatedly say, "John, *you* die—Thompson kill."

But to appease the king was not all that was necessary. In consequence of the insult offered to their prince, the whole tribe held a council in which it was unanimously resolved that Thompson should be put to death in the most cruel manner. I, however, interceded so strenuously with Maquinna for his life, telling him that if my father was killed I was determined not to survive him, that he refused to deliver him up to the vengeance of his people, saying that for John's sake they must consent to let him live. The prince, who, after I had succeeded in calming his father, gave me an account of what had happened, told me that it was wholly out of regard to me, as Thompson was my father, that his life had been spared. If anyone of the tribe should dare to lift a hand against him in anger, he would most certainly be put to death.

Yet even this narrow escape produced not much effect on Thompson or induced him to restrain the violence of his temper. Not many weeks after, he was guilty of a similar indiscretion in striking the eldest son of a chief, who was about eighteen years old, and according to their custom was considered as a *Tyee*, or chief, himself, in consequence of his having provoked him by calling him a white slave. This affair caused great commotion in the village and the tribe was very clamorous for his death, but Maquinna would not consent. I used frequently to remonstrate with him on the imprudence of his conduct and beg him to govern his temper better, telling him it was our duty, since our lives were in the power of these savages, to do nothing to exasperate them.

But all I could say on this point availed little. So bitter was the hate he felt for them, which he was no way backward in

A Mowachaht house, as sketched by John Webber. Once nails became common, a result of trade, houses were no longer dismantled and transported when the tribe moved for the different seasons.

manifesting both by his looks and actions, that he declared he never would submit to their insults, and that he had much rather be killed than be obliged to live among them, adding that he only wished he had a good vessel and some guns and he would destroy the whole of the cursed race. For to a brave sailor like him, who had fought the French and Spaniards with glory, it was a punishment worse than death to be a slave to such a poor, ignorant, despicable set of beings.

As for myself, I thought very differently. After returning thanks to that merciful Being who had in so wonderful a manner softened the hearts of the savages in my favour, I had determined from the first of my capture to adopt a conciliating conduct towards them and conform myself, as far as was in my power, to their customs and mode of thinking, trusting that the same divine goodness that had rescued me from death would not always suffer me to languish in captivity among these heathen. With this view I sought to gain their good will by always endeavouring to assume a cheerful countenance, appearing pleased with their sports and buffoon tricks, making little ornaments for the wives and children of the chiefs, by which means I became quite a favourite with them, and fish-hooks, daggers, &c., for themselves. As a further recommendation to their favour, and what might eventually prove of the utmost importance to us, I resolved to learn their language, which in the course of a few months residence I so far succeeded in acquiring as to be able in general to make myself well understood. I likewise tried to persuade Thompson to learn it as it might prove necessary to him. But he refused, saying that he hated both them and their cursed lingo and would have nothing to do with it.

By pursuing this conciliatory plan, so far did I gain the good will of the savages, particularly the chiefs, that I scarcely ever failed experiencing kind treatment from them, and was received with a smile of welcome at their houses where I was always sure of having something given me to eat, whenever they had it. Many a good meal have I had from them when they themselves were short of provisions and suffering for the want of them. And it was a common practice with me when we had nothing to eat at home, which happened not unfrequently during my stay among them, to go around the village, and on noticing a smoke from any of the houses, which denoted that they were cooking, enter in without ceremony and ask them for something, which I was never refused. Few nations, indeed, are there, so very rude and unfeeling, whom constant mild treatment and an attention to please will not mollify and obtain from them some return of kind attention. The treatment I received from these people may exemplify this for not numerous, even among those calling themselves civilized, are there instances to be found of persons depriving themselves of food to give to a stranger, whatever may be his merits.

seven

Observations on the Nootka

It may perhaps be as well in this place to give a description of Nootka, some accounts of the tribes who were accustomed to visit us, and the manners and customs of the people as far as I hitherto had an opportunity of observing them.

The village of Nootka is situated in between 49 and 50 degrees north latitude at the bottom of Friendly Cove on the west or northwest side. It consists of about twenty houses or huts on a small hill which rises with a gentle ascent from the shore. Friendly Cove, which affords good and secure anchorage for ships close in with the shore, is a small harbour of not more than a quarter or half a mile in length, and about half a mile or three quarters broad, formed by the line of coast on the east, and a long point, or headland, which extends as much as three leagues into the sound in nearly a westerly direction. This, as well as I can judge from what I have seen of it, is in general from one to two miles in breadth and mostly a rocky and unproductive soil with but few trees. The eastern and western shores of this harbour are steep and in many parts rocky, the trees growing quite to the water's edge, but the bottom to the north and northwest is a fine sandy beach of half a mile or more in extent.

From the village to the north and northeast extends a plain, the soil of which is very excellent, and with proper cultivation may be made to produce almost any of our European vegetables. This is but little more than half a mile in breadth and is terminated by the sea coast, which in this place is lined with rocks and reefs and cannot be approached by ships. The coast in the neighbourhood of Nootka is in general low and but little broken into hills and valleys. The soil is good, well covered with fine forests of pine [cedar], spruce, beech, and other trees, and abounds with streams of the finest water, the general appearance being the same for many miles round.

The village is situated on the ground occupied by the Spaniards when they kept a garrison here. The foundations of the church and the governor's house are yet visible, and a few European plants are still to be found, which continue to be self-propagated, such as onions, peas, and turnips. But the two last are quite small, particularly the turnips, which afford us nothing but the tops for eating. The former village stood on the same spot, but the Spaniards, finding it a commodious situation, demolished the houses and forced the inhabitants to retire five or six miles into the country. With great sorrow, as Maquinna told me, did they find themselves compelled to quit their ancient place of residence, but with equal joy did they repossess themselves of it when the Spanish garrison was expelled by the English.

The houses, as I have observed, are above twenty in number, built nearly in a line. These are of different sizes according to the rank or quality of the *Tyee*, or chief, who lives in them, each having one, of which he is considered as the lord. They vary not much in width, being usually from 36 to 40 feet wide, but are of

House frames at Nootka Sound. Nuu-chah-nulth houses were huge, ranging from 40 to 150 feet in length, and were usually placed broadside to the beach.

very different lengths. That of the king, which is much the longest, being about 150 feet, while the smallest, which contain only two families, do not exceed 40 feet in length. The house of the king is also distinguished from the others by being higher.

Their method of building is as follows: they erect in the ground two very large posts at such a distance apart as is intended for the length of the house. On these, which are of equal height and hollowed out at the upper end, they lay a large spar for the ridgepole of the building, or if the length of the house requires it, two or more, supporting their ends by similar upright posts. These spars are sometimes of an almost incredible size, having myself measured one in Maquinna's house which I found to be 100 feet long and 8 feet 4 inches in circumference. At equal distances from these two posts, two others are placed on each

The roof supports for this Nuu-chah-nulth house have human and animal faces carved or painted on the wood.

side to form the width of the building. These are rather shorter than the first, and on them are laid in like manner spars, but of a smaller size, having the upper part hewed flat, with a narrow ridge on the outer side to support the ends of the planks.

The roof is formed of pine planks with a broad feather edge so as to lap well over each other. They are laid lengthwise from the ridgepole in the centre to the beams at the sides, after which the top is covered with planks of eight feet broad, which form a kind of covering projecting so far over the ends of the planks that form the roof as completely to exclude the rain. On these they lay large stones to prevent their being displaced by the wind. The ends of the planks are not secured to the beams on which they are laid by any fastening. In a high storm I have often known all the men obliged to turn out and go upon the roof to prevent them from being blown off, carrying large stones and pieces of rock with them to secure the boards, always stripping themselves naked on these occasions, whatever may be the severity of the weather, to prevent their garments from being wet and muddied as these storms are almost always accompanied with heavy rains.

The sides of their houses are much more open and exposed to the weather. This proceeds from their not being so easily made close as the roof, being built with planks of about ten feet long and four or five wide, which they place between stanchions or small posts of the height of the roof. Of these there are four to each range of boards, two at each end, and so near each other as to leave space enough for admitting a plank. The planks, or boards, which they make use of for building their houses and for other uses, they procure of different lengths as occasion requires by splitting them out, with hard wooden wedges, from pine logs and afterwards dubbing them down with their chisels, with much patience, to the thickness wanted, rendering them quite smooth.

There is but one entrance; this is placed usually at the end, though sometimes in the middle as was that of Maquinna's. Through the middle of the building from one end to the other runs a passage of about eight or nine feet broad, on each side of which live the several families that occupy it, each having its particular fireplace, but without any kind of wall or separation to mark their respective limits; the chief having his apartment at the upper end, and the next in rank opposite on the other side. They have no other floor than the ground. The fireplace or hearth consists of a number of stones loosely put together, but they are wholly without a chimney. Nor is there any opening left in the roof. Whenever a fire is made, the plank immediately over it is thrust aside by means of a pole to give vent to the smoke.

The height of the houses in general, from the ground to the centre of the roof, does not exceed ten feet; that of Maquinna's was not far from fourteen. The spar forming the ridgepole of the latter was painted in red and black circles alternately by way of ornament. The large posts that supported it had their tops curiously wrought or carved so as to represent human heads of a monstrous size, which were painted in their manner. These were not, however, considered as objects of adoration but merely as ornaments.

The furniture of these people is very simple, and consists only of boxes in which they put their clothes, furs, and such things as they hold most valuable; tubs for keeping their provision of spawn and blubber in; trays from which they eat; baskets for their dried fish and other purposes; and bags made of bark matting, of which they also make their beds, spreading a piece of it upon the ground when they lie down, and using no other bed covering than their garments. The boxes are of pine [cedar], with a top that shuts over, and instead of nails or pegs are fastened with flexible twigs. They are extremely smooth and high polished and sometimes ornamented with rows of very small white shells. The tubs are of a square form, secured in the like manner, and of various sizes, some being extremely large, having seen them that were six feet long by four broad and five deep. The trays are hollowed out with their chisels from a solid block of wood, and the baskets and mats are made from the bark of trees.

From this they likewise make the cloth for their garments, in the following manner: A quantity of this bark is taken and put into fresh water, where it is kept for a fortnight to give it time to completely soften. It is then taken out and beaten upon a plank with an instrument made of bone or some very hard wood, having grooves or hollows on one side of it, care being taken to keep the mass constantly moistened with water in order to separate with more ease the hard and woody from the soft and fibrous parts which, when completed, they parcel out into skeins, like thread. These they lay in the air to bleach, and afterwards dye them black or red as suits their fancies, their natural colour being a pale yellow. In order to form the cloth the women, by whom the whole of this process is performed, take a certain number of these skeins and twist them together by rolling them with their hands upon their knees into hard rolls, which are afterwards connected by means of a strong thread made for the purpose.

Their dress usually consists of but a single garment, which is a loose cloak or mantle (called *kutsack*) in one piece, reaching nearly to the feet. This is tied loosely over the right or left shoulder

The *kutsack*.

so as to leave the arms at full liberty.

Those of the common people are painted red with ochre, the better to keep out the rain, but the chiefs wear them of their native colour, which is a pale yellow, ornamenting them with borders of the sea otter skin, a kind of grey cloth made of the hair of some animal which they procure from the tribes to the south, or their own cloth wrought or painted with various figures in red or black, representing men's heads, the sun and moon, fish and animals, which are frequently executed with much skill. They have also a girdle of the same kind for securing this mantle, or *kutsack*, around them, which is in general still more highly ornamented, and serves them to wear their daggers and knives in.

In winter, however, they sometimes make use of an additional garment which is a kind of hood with a hole in it for the purpose of admitting the head, and falls over the breast and back as low as the shoulders. This is bordered both at top and bottom with fur, and is never worn except when they go out.

The garments of the women vary not essentially from those of the men, the mantle having holes in it for the purpose of admitting the arms, and being tied close under the chin instead of over the shoulder.

The chiefs have also mantles of the sea otter skin, but these are only put on upon extraordinary occasions, and one that is

Cedar blankets, in the process of being made (above) and worn (below).
The bark was soaked for three days in salt water, then worked to become
soft and pliable and more like a fabric.

made from the skin of a certain large animal which is brought from the south by the Wickanninish and Kla-iz-zarts. This they prepare by dressing it in warm water, scraping off the hair and what flesh adheres to it carefully with sharp mussel shells, and spreading it out in the sun to dry, on a wooden frame, so as to preserve the shape. When dressed in this manner it becomes perfectly white and as pliable as the best deer's leather, but almost as thick again. They then paint it in different figures with such paints as they usually employ in decorating their persons. These figures mostly represent human heads, canoes employed in catching whales, &c.

This skin is called *metamelth* and is probably got from an animal of the moose kind [elk]. It is highly prized by these people, is their great war dress, and is only worn when they wish to make the best possible display of themselves. Strips or bands of it, painted as above, are also sometimes used by them for girdles or the bordering of their cloaks, and also for bracelets and ankle ornaments by some of the inferior class.

On their heads when they go out upon any excursion, particularly whaling or fishing, they wear a kind of cap or bonnet, in form not unlike a large sugar loaf with the top cut off. This is made of the same materials as their cloth, but is in general of a closer texture, and by way of tassel has a long strip of the skin of the *metamelth* attached to it, covered with rows of small white shells or beads. Those worn by the common people are painted entirely red, the chiefs having theirs of different colours. The one worn by the king and which serves to designate him from all the others is longer and broader at the bottom; the top, instead of being flat, having upon it an ornament in the figure of a small urn. It is also of a much finer texture than the others and plaited or wrought in black and white stripes with the representation in front of a canoe in pursuit of a whale with the harpooner standing in the prow prepared to strike. This bonnet is called *seeya-poks*.

Their mode of living is very simple—their food consisting almost wholly of fish, or fish spawn fresh or dried; the blubber of the whale, seal, or sea-cow; mussels, clams, and berries of various kinds; all of which are eaten with a profusion of train oil for sauce, not excepting even the most delicate fruit, as strawberries and raspberries. With so little variety in their food, no great variety can be expected in their cookery.

Of this, indeed, they may be said to know but two methods, viz. by boiling and steaming. Even the latter is not very frequently practised by them. Their mode of boiling is as follows: into one of their tubs they pour water sufficient to cook the quantity of provision wanted. A number of heated stones are then put in to make it boil. The salmon or other fish are put in without any other preparation than sometimes cutting off the heads, tails, and fins, the boiling in the meantime being kept up by the application of the hot stones, after which it is left to cook until the whole is nearly reduced to one mass. It is then taken out and distributed in the trays. In a similar manner they cook their blubber and spawn, smoked or dried fish, and in fine, almost everything they eat, nothing going down with them like broth.

When they cook their fish by steam, which are usually the heads, tails, and fins of the salmon, cod, and halibut, a large fire is kindled, upon which they place a bed of stones which, when the wood is burnt down, becomes perfectly heated. Layers of green leaves or pine boughs are then placed upon the stones, and the fish, clams, &c., being laid upon them, water is poured over them and the whole closely covered with mats to keep in the steam. This is much the best mode of cooking, and clams and mussels done in this manner are really excellent. These, as I have said, may be considered as their only kinds of cookery, though I have in a very few instances known them dress the roe or spawn of the salmon and the herring, when first taken, in a different manner. This was by roasting them, the former being supported between two split pieces of pine, and the other having a sharp stick run through it, with one end fixed in the ground. Sprats are also roasted by them in this way, a number being spitted on one stick, and this kind of food, with a little salt, would be found no contemptible eating even to a European.

At their meals they seat themselves upon the ground with their feet curled up under them, around their trays, which are generally about three feet long by one broad, and from six to eight inches deep. In eating they make use of nothing but their fingers, except for the soup or oil which they lade out with clam shells. Around one of these trays from four to six persons will seat themselves, constantly dipping in their fingers or clam shells, one after the other.

The king and chiefs alone have separate trays from which no one is permitted to eat with them except the queen or principal wife of the chief. Whenever the king or one of the chiefs wishes to distinguish any of his people with a special mark of favour on these occasions, he calls him and gives him some of the choice bits from his tray.

The slaves eat at the same time and of the same provisions, faring in this respect as well as their masters, being seated with the family and only feeding from separate trays.

Whenever a feast is given by the king or any of the chiefs, there is a person who acts as a master of ceremonies and whose business it is to receive the guests as they enter the house and point out to them their respective seats, which is regulated with great punctiliousness as regards rank; the king occupying the highest or the seat of honour, his son or brother sitting next him, and so on with the chiefs according to their quality; the private persons belonging to the same family being always placed together to prevent any confusion. The women are seldom invited to their feasts, and only at those times when a general invitation is given to the village.

As whenever they cook they always calculate to have an abundance for all the guests, a profusion in this respect being considered as the highest luxury, much more is usually set before them than they can eat. That which is left in the king's tray he sends to his house for his family, by one of his slaves, as do the chiefs theirs. Those who eat from the same tray and who generally belong to the same family take it home as common stock, or each one receives his portion, which is distributed on the spot. This custom appeared very singular to my companion and myself, and it was a most awkward thing for us at first to have to lug home with us, in our hands or arms, the blubber or fish that we received at these times. But we soon became reconciled to it and were very glad of an opportunity to do it.

In point of personal appearance, the people of Nootka are among the best looking of any of the tribes that I have seen. The men are in general from about five feet six to five feet eight inches in height; remarkably straight, of a good form, robust, and strong, with their limbs in general well turned and proportioned excepting the legs and feet, which are clumsy and ill formed, owing no doubt to their practice of sitting on them, though I have seen instances in which they were very well shaped; this defect is more particularly apparent in the women, who are for the most part of the time within doors and constantly sitting while employed in their cooking and other occupations.

The only instance of deformity that I saw among them was a man of dwarfish stature. He was 30 years old and but three feet three inches high. He had, however, no other defect than this diminutive, being well made and as strong and able to bear fatigue as what they were in general.

Their complexion, when freed from the paint and oil with which their skins are generally covered, is a brown, somewhat inclining to a copper cast. The shape of the face is oval; the features are tolerably regular, the lips being thin and the teeth very white and even. Their eyes are black but rather small, and the nose pretty well formed, being neither flat nor very prominent. Their hair is black, long, and coarse, but they have no beard, completely extirpating it, as well as the hair from their bodies, Maquinna being the only exception, who suffered his beard to grow on his upper lip, in the manner of mustachios, which was considered as a mark of dignity.

As to the women, they are much whiter, many of them not being darker than those in some of the southern parts of Europe. They are in general very well looking and some quite handsome. Maquinna's favourite wife in particular, who was a Wickanninish princess, would be considered as a beautiful woman in any country. She was uncommonly well formed, tall, and of a majestic appearance: her skin remarkably fair for one of these people, with considerable colour, her features handsome and her eyes black, soft, and languishing. Her hair was very long, thick, and black, as is that of the females in general, which is much softer than that of the men.

In this they take much pride, frequently oiling and plaiting it carefully into two broad plaits, tying the ends with a strip of the cloth of the country and letting it hang down on each side of the face.

The women keep their garments much neater and cleaner than the men and are extremely modest in their deportment and dress; their mantle, or *kutsack,* which is longer than that of the men, reaching quite to their feet and completely enveloping them, being tied close under the chin and bound with a girdle of the same cloth or of sea otter skin around their waists. It has also loose sleeves which reach to the elbows. Though fond of ornamenting their persons, they are by no means so partial to paint as the men, merely colouring their eyebrows black and drawing a bright red stripe from each corner of the mouth towards the ear.

Their ornaments consist chiefly of earrings, necklaces, bracelets, rings for the fingers and ankles, and small nose jewels (the latter are, however, wholly confined to the wives of the king or chiefs). These are principally made out of copper or brass, highly polished and of various forms and sizes; the nose jewel is usually a small white shell or bead suspended to a thread. The wives of the common people frequently wear, for bracelets and ankle rings, strips of the country cloth or skin of the *metamelth* painted in figures, and those of the king or principal chiefs, bracelets and necklaces consisting of a number of strings of *i-whaw* [dentalia shells], an article much prized by them, and which makes a very handsome appearance.

This *i-whaw,* as they term it, is a kind of shell of a dazzling whiteness, and as smooth as ivory. It is of a cylindrical form, in a slight degree curved, about the size of a goose quill, hollow, three inches in length and gradually tapering to a point, which is broken off by the natives as it is taken from the water. This they afterwards string upon threads of bark and sell it by the fathom. It forms a kind of circulating medium among these nations, five fathoms being considered as the price of a slave, their most valuable species of property. It is principally obtained from the Ai-tiz-zarts, a people living about 30 or 40 miles to the

Men were often much more ornamented than the women.

northward, who collect it from the reefs and sunken rocks with which their coast abounds, though it is also brought in considerable quantity from the south.

Their mode of taking it has been thus described to me. To one end of a pole is fastened a piece of plank in which a considerable number of pine pegs are inserted, made sharp at the ends. Above the plank, in order to sink it, a stone or some weight is tied, and the other end of the pole suspended to a long rope. This is let down perpendicularly by the *i-whaw* fishers in those places where that substance is found, which are usually from 50 to 60 fathoms deep. On finding the bottom they raise the pole up a few feet and let it fall; this they repeat a number of times as if sounding, when they draw it up and take off the *i-whaw*, which is found adhering to the points. This method of procuring it is very laborious and fatiguing, especially as they seldom take more than two or three of these shells at a time, and frequently none.

Though the women, as I have said, make but little use of paint, the very reverse is the case with the men. They place their principal pride in decorating their heads and faces, and none of our most fashionable beaus, when preparing for a grand ball, can be more particular. I have known Maquinna, after having been employed for more than an hour in painting his face, rub the whole off and recommence the operation anew when it did not entirely please him.

The manner in which they paint themselves frequently varies according to the occasion, but it oftener is the mere dictate of whim. The most usual method is to paint the eyebrows black, in form of a half moon, and the face red in small squares, with the arms and legs and part of the body red. Sometimes one half of the face is painted red in squares, and the other black; at others, dotted with red spots, or red and black instead of squares, with a variety of other devices, such as painting one half of the face and body red, and the other black.

But a method of painting which they sometimes employed, and which they were much more particular in, was by laying on the face a quantity of bear's grease of about one eighth of an inch thick. This they raised up into ridges resembling a small bead in joiner's work, with a stick prepared for the purpose, and then painted them red, which gave the face a very singular appearance.

On extraordinary occasions, the king and principal chiefs used to strew over their faces, after painting, a fine black shining powder, procured from some mineral, as Maquinna told me it was got from the rocks. This they call *pelpelth* [mica], and value it highly, as, in their opinion, it serves to set off their looks to great advantage, glittering, especially in the sun, like silver. This article is brought them in bags by the Newchemass, a very savage nation who live way to the north, from whom they likewise receive a superior kind of red paint, a species of very fine and rich ochre, which they hold in much estimation.

Notwithstanding this custom of painting themselves, they make it an invariable practice, both in summer and winter, to bathe once a day and sometimes oftener. But as the paint is put on with oil, it is not much discomposed thereby, and whenever they wish to wash it off, they repair to some piece of fresh water and scour themselves with sand or rushes.

In dressing their heads on occasion of a festival or visit, they are full as particular, and almost as long, as in painting. The hair, after being well oiled, is carefully gathered upon the top of the head and secured by a piece of pine or spruce bough with the green leaves upon it. After having it properly fixed in this manner, the king and principal chiefs used to strew all over it the white down obtained from a species of large brown eagle which abounds on this coast, which they are very particular in arranging so as not to have a single feather out of place, occasionally wetting the hair to make it adhere. This, together with the bough, which is sometimes of considerable size, and stuck over with feathers by means of turpentine, gives them a very singular and grotesque appearance, which they, however, think very becoming. The first thing they do on learning of the arrival of strangers is to go and decorate themselves in this manner.

The men also wear bracelets of painted leather or copper, and large earrings of the latter. But the ornament on which they appear to set the most value is the nose-jewel, if such an appellation may be given to the wooden stick that some of them employ for this purpose. The king and chiefs, however, wear them of a different form, being either small pieces of polished copper or brass, of which I made many for them in the shape of hearts and diamonds, or a twisted conical shell about half an inch in length of a blueish colour and very bright, which is brought from the south. These are suspended by a small wire or string to the hole, in the gristle of the nose, which is formed in infancy by boring it with a pin, the hole being afterwards enlarged by the repeated insertion of wooden pegs of an increased size until it becomes about the diameter of a pipe stem, though some have them of a size nearly sufficient to admit the little finger.

The common class, who cannot readily procure the more expensive jewels that I have mentioned, substitute for them, usually, a smooth round stick, some of which are of an almost incredible length. I have seen them projecting not less than eight or nine inches beyond the face on each side. This is made fast or secured in its place by little wedges on each side of it. These sprit-sail-yard fellows, as my messmate used to call them, when rigged out in this manner made quite a strange show. It was his delight, whenever he saw one of them coming towards us with an air of consequence proportioned to the length of his stick, to put up his hand suddenly as he was passing him so as to strike the stick, in order, as he said, to brace him up sharp to the wind. This used to make them very angry, but nothing was more remote from Thompson's ideas than the wish to cultivate their favour.

The natives of Nootka appear to have but little inclination for the chase, though some of them were expert marksmen and used sometimes to shoot ducks and geese, but the seal and the sea otter form the principal objects of their hunting, particularly the latter.

Of this animal, so much noted for its valuable skin, the following description may not be uninteresting: The sea otter is nearly five feet in length, exclusive of the tail, which is about twelve inches and is very thick and broad where it joins the body, but gradually tapers to the end, which is tipped with white. The colour of the rest is a shining silky black, with the exception of a broad white stripe on the top of the head. Nothing can be more beautiful than one of these animals when seen swimming, especially when on the lookout for any object. At such times it raises its head quite above the surface, and the contrast between the shining black and the white, together with its sharp ears and a long tuft of hair rising from the middle of its forehead, which look like three small horns, render it quite a novel and attractive object. They are in general very tame and will permit a canoe or boat to approach very near before they dive. I was told, however, that they are become much more shy since they have been accustomed to shoot them with muskets than when they used only arrows.

Sea otters relaxing (above) and hunted (below). The best time to hunt sea otters was during calm weather, when bubbles coming up to the surface signalled their presence beneath the surface. When the unsuspecting otter rose for air, it would be greeted by arrows made of fir or cedar. The tips were usually fashioned from bone.

The skin is held in great estimation in China, more especially that of the tail, the fur of which is finer and closer set than that on the body. This is always cut off and sold separately by the natives. The value of a skin is determined by its size, that being considered as a prime skin which will reach, in length, from a man's chin to his feet.

A whaler's hat. Archaeological research has uncovered similar hats up to 3,000 years old, marking the Nuu-chah-nulth as longstanding occupants of Nootka Sound. This hat is made from spruce roots as well as cedar bark.

The food of the sea otter is fish, which he is very dexterous in taking, being an excellent swimmer, with feet webbed like those of a goose. They appear to be wholly confined to the sea-coast, at least to the salt water. They have usually three or four young at a time, but I know not how often they breed, nor in what places they deposit their young, though I have frequently seen them swimming around the mother when no larger than rats. The flesh is eaten by the natives, cooked in their usual mode by boiling, and is far preferable to that of the seal of which they make much account.

But if not great hunters, there are few people more expert in fishing. Their lines are generally made from the sinew of the whale and are extremely strong. For the hook, they usually make use of a straight piece of hard wood, in the lower part of which is inserted and well secured, with thread or whale sinew, a bit of bone made very sharp at the point and bearded; but I used to make for them hooks from iron, which they preferred, not only

A two-pronged harpoon used for killing sea animals.

as being less liable to break, but more certain of securing the fish. Cod, halibut, and other seafish were not only caught by them with hooks, but even salmon.

To take this latter fish, they practise the following method: One person seats himself in a small canoe, and baiting his hook with a sprat, which they are always careful to procure as fresh as possible, fastens his line to the handle of the paddle. This, as he plies it in the water, keeps the fish in constant motion so as to give it the appearance of life, which the salmon seeing, leaps at it and is instantly hooked and, by a sudden and dexterous motion of the paddle, drawn on board. I have known some of the natives to take no less than eight to ten salmon of a morning in this manner, and have seen from 20 to 30 canoes at a time in Friendly Cove thus employed.

They are likewise little less skilful in taking the whale. This they kill with a kind of javelin or harpoon, thus constructed and fitted: The barbs are formed of bone, which are sharpened on the outer side and hollowed within for the purpose of forming a socket for the staff. These are then secured firmly together with whale sinew, the point being fitted so as to receive a piece of mussel shell, which is ground to a very sharp edge and secured in its place by means of turpentine. To this head, or prong, is fastened a strong line of whale sinew about nine feet in length, to the end of which is tied a bark rope from 50 to 60 fathoms long, having from 20 to 30 seal-skin floats, or buoys, attached to it at certain intervals in order to check the motion of the whale and obstruct his diving.

In the socket of the harpoon, a staff or pole of about ten feet long, gradually tapering from the middle to each end, is placed. This the harpooner holds in his hand in order to strike the whale, and immediately detaches it as soon as the fish is struck. The whale is considered as the king's fish, and no other person, when he is present, is permitted to touch him until the royal harpoon has first drawn his blood, however near he may approach. It would be considered almost as sacrilege for any of the common people to strike a whale before he is killed, particularly if any of the chiefs should be present. They also kill the porpoise and sea cow [sea lion] with harpoons, but this inferior game is not interdicted the lower class.

With regard to their canoes, some of the handsomest to be found on the whole coast are made at Nootka, though very fine ones are brought by the Wickanninish and the Kla-iz-zarts, who have them more highly ornamented. They are of all sizes, from such as are capable of holding only one person to their largest war canoes, which will carry 40 men and are extremely light. Of these, the largest of any that I ever saw was one belonging to Maquinna, which I measured and found to be 42 feet 6 inches in length at the bottom, and 46 feet from stem to stern.

These are made of pine [cedar] hollowed out from a tree with their chisels solely, which are about three inches broad and six in length, and set into a handle of very hard wood. This instrument was formerly made of flint or some hard stone ground down to as sharp an edge as possible, but since they have learned the use of iron, they have almost all of them of that metal. Instead of a mallet for striking this chisel, they make use of a smooth round stone, which they hold in the palm of the hand. With this same awkward instrument they not only excavate their canoes and trays and smooth their planks, but also cut down such trees as they want, either for building, fuel, or other purposes, a labour mostly done by their slaves.

The falling of trees as practised by them is a slow and most tedious process, three of them being generally from two to three days in cutting down a large one. Yet so attached were they to their own method that, notwithstanding they saw Thompson frequently with one of our axes, of which there was a number saved, fall a tree in less time than they could have gone round it with their chisels, still they could not be persuaded to make use of them.

After hollowing out their canoes, which they do very neatly, they fashion the outside and slightly burn it for the purpose of removing any splinters

This example of a Mowachaht canoe was 55 feet long and 6 feet deep. It was supposed to be a sort of ferry to Neah Bay across the Strait of Juan de Fuca. However, it was too large to handle properly.

or small points that might obstruct its passage through the water, after which they rub it over thoroughly, with rushes or coarse mats, in order to smooth it, which not only renders it almost as smooth as glass, but forms a better security for it from the weather. This operation of burning and rubbing down the bottoms of their canoes is practised as often as they acquire any considerable degree of roughness from use. The outside, by this means becomes quite black, and to complete their work they paint the inside a bright red with ochre or some other similar substance. The prows and sterns are almost always ornamented with figures of ducks or some other kind of bird, the former being so fashioned as to represent the head and the latter the tail. These are separate pieces from the canoe and are fastened to it with small flexible twigs or bark cord.

Some of these canoes, particularly those employed in whaling, which will hold about ten men, are ornamented within about two inches below the gunwale with two parallel lines on each side of very small white shells running fore and aft, which has a very pretty effect. Their war canoes have no ornament of this kind but are painted on the outside with figures in white chalk representing eagles, whales, human heads, &c. They are very dexterous in the use of their paddles, which are very neatly wrought and are five feet long with a short handle and a blade seven inches broad in the middle, tapering to a sharp point. With these they will make a canoe skim very swiftly on the water with scarcely any noise, while they keep time to the stroke of the paddle with their songs.

With regard to these they have a number which they sing on various occasions, as war, whaling, and fishing, at their marriages and feasts, and at public festivals or solemnities. The language of most of these appears to be very different, in many respects, from that used in their common conversation, which leads me to believe either that they have a different mode of expressing themselves in poetry, or that they borrow their songs from their neighbours. What the more particularly induces me to the latter opinion is that whenever any of the Newchemass, a people from the northward and who speak a very different language, arrived, they used to tell me that they expected a new song and were almost always sure to have one. Their tunes are generally soft and plaintive, and though not possessing great variety, are not deficient in harmony. Their singing is generally accompanied with several rude kinds of instrumental music, among the most prominent of which is a kind of drum. This is nothing more than a long plank hollowed out on the underside and made quite thin, which is beat upon by a stick of about a foot long and renders a sound not unlike beating on the head of an empty cask, but much louder. But the two most favourite instruments are the rattle and the pipe, or whistle. These are, however, only used by the king, the chiefs, or some particular persons. The former is made of dried seal skin so as to represent a fish, and is filled with a number of small smooth pebbles, has a short handle, and is painted red. The whistle is made of bone, generally the leg of a deer. It is short but emits a very shrill sound. They have likewise another kind of music, which they make use of in dancing, in the manner of castanets. This is produced by a number of mussel or cockle shells tied together and shaken to a kind of tune, which is accompanied with the voice.

Their slaves, as I have observed, form their most valuable species of property. These are of both sexes, being either captives taken by themselves in war or purchased from the neighbouring tribes, and who reside in the same house, forming as it were a part of the family, are usually kindly treated, eat of the same food, and live as well as their masters. They are compelled, however, at times to labour severely, as not only all the menial offices are performed by them, such as bringing water, cutting wood, and a variety of others, but they are obliged to make the canoes, to assist in building and repairing the houses, to supply their masters with fish, and to attend them to war and to fight for them.

None but the king and chiefs have slaves, the common people being prevented from holding them either from their inability to purchase them, or as I am the rather inclined to think, from its being considered as the privilege of the former alone to have them, especially as all those made prisoners in war belong either to the king or the chiefs, who have captured them, each one holding such as have been taken by himself or his slaves. There is probably, however, some little distinction in favour of the king, who is always the commander of the expedition. Maquinna had nearly 50, male and female, in his house, a number constituting about one half of its inhabitants, comprehending those obtained by war and purchase, whereas none of the other chiefs had more than 12.

The females are employed principally in manufacturing cloth, in cooking, collecting berries, &c., and with regard to food and living in general have not a much harder lot than their mistresses, the principal difference consisting in these poor unfortunate creatures being considered as free to anyone, their masters prostituting them whenever they think proper for the purpose of gain. In this way, many of them are brought on board the ships and offered to the crews, from whence an opinion appears to have been formed by some of our navigators, injurious to the chastity of their females, than which nothing can be more generally untrue, as perhaps in no part of the world is that virtue more prized.

The houses at Nootka, as already stated, are about twenty, without comprising those inhabited by the Klahars, a small tribe that has been conquered and incorporated into that of Nootka, though they must be considered as in a state of vassalage as they are not permitted to have any chiefs among them and live by themselves in a cluster of small houses at a little distance from the village. The Nootka tribe, which consists of about 500 warriors, is not only more numerous than almost any of the neighbouring tribes, but far exceeds them in the strength and martial spirit of its people. In fact, there are but few nations within 100 miles either to the north or south but are considered as tributary to them.

eight

Observations on Neighbouring Tribes

In giving some account of the tribes that were accustomed to visit Nootka, I shall commence at the southward with the Kla-iz-zarts, and the Wickanninish, premising that in point of personal appearance there prevails a wonderful diversity between the various tribes on the coast, with the exception of the feet and legs, which are badly shaped in almost all of them from their practice of sitting on them.

The Kla-iz-zarts are a numerous and powerful tribe, living nearly 300 miles to the south, and are said to consist of more than a thousand warriors. They appear to be more civilized than any of the others, being better and more neatly dressed, more mild and affable in their manners, remarkable for their

A Kwakiutl warrior. Even though not mentioned by
Jewitt, the Kwakiutl are related linguistically to the
Nuu-chah-nulth. Because of objections to the Kwakiutl
name, these people propose the name Kwa-kwa-
ka'wakw, which means "people who speak Kwakwala."

sprightliness and vivacity, and celebrated for their singing and
dancing. They exhibit also great marks of improvement in
whatever is wrought by them. Their canoes, though not superior
to those of Nootka in point of form and lightness, being more
highly ornamented, and their weapons and tools of every kind
have a much higher finish and display more skill in the
workmanship.

Their cast of countenance is very different from that of the
Nootkians, their faces being very broad, with a less prominent

nose and smaller eyes, and the top of the head flattened as if it had been pressed down with a weight. Their complexion is also much fairer, and their stature shorter, though they are well formed and strongly set. They have a custom which appears to be peculiar to them, as I never observed it in any of the other tribes, which is to pluck out not only their beards and the hair from their bodies, but also their eyebrows, so as not to leave a vestige remaining. They were also in general more skilful in painting and decorating themselves, and I have seen some of them with no less than a dozen holes in each of their ears, to which were suspended strings of small beads about two inches in length.

Their language is the same as spoken at Nootka, but their pronunciation is much more hoarse and guttural. These people are not only very expert in whaling, but are great hunters of the sea otter and other animals with which their country is said to abound, as the *metamelth*, a large animal of the deer kind, the skin of which I have already spoken of; another of a light grey colour, with very fine hair from which they manufacture a handsome cloth; the beaver; and a species of large wild cat, or tyger cat [cougar].

The Wickanninish, their neighbours on the north, are about 200 miles from Nootka. They are a robust, strong, and warlike people, but considered by the Nootkians as their inferiors in courage. This tribe is more numerous than that of Nootka, amounting to between 600 and 700 warriors. Though not so civilized as the Kla-iz-zarts, and less skilful in their manufactures, like them they employ themselves in hunting as well as in whaling and fishing. Their faces are broad, but less so than the Kla-iz-zarts, with a darker complexion and a much less open and pleasing expression of countenance, while their heads present a very different form, being pressed in at the sides and lengthened towards the top, somewhat in the shape of a sugar loaf. These people are very frequent visitors at Nootka, a close friendship subsisting between the two nations, Maquinna's *arcomah*, or queen, Y-ya-tintla-no, being the daughter of the Wickanninish king.

The Kla-oo-quates adjoining them on the north are much less numerous, their force not exceeding 400 fighting men. They are also behind them in the arts of life. These are a fierce, bold, and enterprising people, and there were none that visited Nootka whom Maquinna used to be more on his guard against, or viewed with so much suspicion.

The Hesquiaht are about the same number; these are considered as tributary to Maquinna. Their coast abounds with rivers, creeks, and marshes.

To the north, the nearest tribe of any importance is the Ai-tiz-zarts. These, however, do not exceed 300 warriors. In appearance they greatly resemble the people of Nootka, to whom they are considered as tributary, their manners, dress, and style of living also being very similar. They reside at about 40 miles distance up the sound. A considerable way farther to the northward are the Cay-u-quets. These are a much more numerous tribe than that of Nootka, but thought by the latter to be deficient in courage and martial spirit, Maquinna having frequently told me that their hearts were little like those of birds.

There are also both at the north and south many other intervening tribes, but in general small in number and insignificant, all of whom, as well as the above mentioned, speak the same language. But the Newchemass, who come from a great way to the northward and from some distance inland, as I was told by Maquinna, speak quite a different language, although it is well understood by those of Nootka.

These were the most savage looking and ugly men that I ever saw, their complexion being much darker, their stature shorter, and their hair coarser than that of the other nations, and their dress and appearance dirty in an extreme. They wear their beards long, like Jews, and have a very morose and surly countenance. Their usual dress is a *kutsack* made of wolf skin, with a number of the tails attached to it, of which I have seen no less than ten on one garment, hanging from the top to the bottom. They sometimes wear a similar mantle of bark cloth, of a much coarser texture than that of Nootka, the original colour of which appears to be the same, though from their very great filthiness it was almost impossible to discover what it had been. Their mode of dressing their hair also varies essentially from that of the other

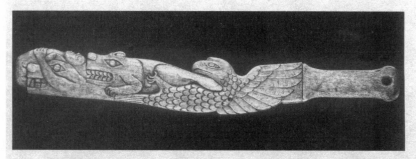

A *cheetoolth* (war club), although a good weapon, was meant to intimidate adversaries and take them as slaves rather than to kill them.

tribes, for they suffer that on the back of the head to hang loose, and bind the other over their foreheads in the manner of a fillet, with a strip of their country cloth, ornamented with small white shells.

Their weapons are the *cheetoolth*, or war club, which is made from whale bone; daggers; bows and arrows; and a kind of spear pointed with bone or copper. They brought with them no furs for sale, excepting a few wolf skins, their merchandise consisting principally of the black shining mineral called *pelpelth*, the fine red paint which they carefully kept in close mat bags, some small dried salmon, clams, and roes of fish, with, occasionally, a little coarse matting cloth. They were accustomed to remain a much longer time at Nootka than the other tribes in order to recover from the fatigue of a long journey, part of which was over land, and on these occasions taught their songs to our savages.

The trade of most of the other tribes with Nootka was principally train oil, seal or whale's blubber, fish fresh or dried, herring or salmon spawn, clams and mussels, the *yama* (a species of fruit [salal berry] which is pressed and dried), cloth, sea otter skins, and slaves. From the Ai-tiz-zarts and the Cay-u-quets, particularly the former, the best *i-whaw* and in the greatest quantities was obtained. The Hesquiahts furnished us with wild ducks and geese, particularly the latter. The Wickanninish and Kla-iz-zarts brought to market many slaves, the best sea otter skins, great quantities of oil, whale sinew, and cakes of *yama*, highly ornamented canoes, some *i-whaw*, red ochre, and *pelpelth* of an inferior quality to that obtained from the Newchemass, but particularly the so-much-valued *metamelth* and an excellent root called by the Kla-iz-zarts *quawnoose* [edible camas]. This is the size of a small onion, but rather longer, being of a tapering form like a pear, and of a brownish colour. It is cooked by steam, is always brought in baskets ready prepared for eating, and is in truth a very fine vegetable, being sweet, mealy, and of a most

Visiting tribes were sure to keep some of their members sleeping in the canoes on shore to prevent theft. These are Kwakiutl canoes.

agreeable flavour. It was highly esteemed by the natives, who used to eat it as they did everything else, with train oil. From the Kla-iz-zarts was also received, though in no great quantity, a cloth manufactured by them from the fur already spoken of, which feels like wool and is of a grey colour.

Many of the articles thus brought, particularly the provisions, were considered as presents or tributary offerings, but this must be viewed as little more than a nominal acknowledgement of superiority, as they rarely failed to get the full amount of the value of their presents. I have known eighteen of the great tubs in which they keep their provisions filled with spawn brought in this way. On these occasions a great feast is always made, to which not only the strangers but the whole village, men, women, and children, are generally invited. I have seen five of the largest tubs employed at such time in cooking at the king's house. At these feasts they generally indulge in eating to an excess, making up in this respect for their want of inebriating liquors, which they know no method of preparing in any form, their only drink being water.

Whenever they came to visit or trade, it was their general custom to stop a few miles distant, under the lee of some bluff or rock, and rig themselves out in their best manner by painting and dressing their heads. On their first coming on shore, they were invited to eat by the king, when they brought to him such articles as he wanted, after which the rest of the inhabitants were permitted to purchase, the strangers being careful to keep them in their canoes until sold, under strict guard to prevent their being stolen, the disposition of these people for thieving being so great that it is necessary to keep a watchful eye upon them.

This was their usual mode of traffic, but whenever they wished to purchase any particular object, as, for instance, a certain slave or some other thing of which they were very desirous, the canoe that came for this purpose would lie off at a little distance from the shore. A kind of ambassador, or representative of the king or chief by whom it was sent, dressed in the best manner and with his head covered with the white down, would rise and, after making known the object of his mission in a pompous speech, hold up specimens of such articles as he was instructed to offer in payment, mentioning the number or quantity of each. If the bargain was concluded, the exchange was immediately made.

On their visits of friendship or traffic, the chiefs alone used to sleep on shore, generally at the house of the king or head chief, the others passing the night on board of their canoes, which was done not only for the preservation of their property, but because they were not permitted to remain on shore, lest they might excite some disturbance or commit depredations.

All these people generally go armed, the common class wearing only a dagger, suspended from their neck behind with a string of *metamelth*, and sometimes thrust in their girdles.

The chiefs, in addition to the dagger, carry the *cheetoolth*, or war-club, suspended in the same manner beneath their mantles. This in the hands of a strong man is a powerful weapon, in the management of which some of the older chiefs are very dexterous. It is made from the bone of a whale and is very heavy. The blade is about eighteen inches long and three broad, till it approaches near the point, where it expands to the breadth of four inches. In the middle, from whence it slopes off gradually to an edge on each side, it is from one to two inches in thickness. This blade is usually covered with figures of the sun and moon, a man's head, &c., and the hilt, which is made to represent the head of a man or some animal, is curiously set with small white shells and has a band of *metamelth* fastened to it in order to sling it over the shoulder.

Some of the tribes have also a kind of spear, headed with copper or the bone of the stingray, which is a dangerous weapon. This is, however, not usual and is only carried by the chiefs. The bow and arrow are still used by a few, but since the introduction of firearms among them, this weapon has been mostly laid aside.

nine

Living as Captives

But to return to our unhappy situation. Though my comrade and myself fared as well, and even better than we could have expected among these people, considering their customs and mode of living, yet our fears lest no ship would come to our release and that we should never more behold a Christian country were to us a source of constant pain. Our principal consolation in this gloomy state was to go on Sundays, whenever the weather would permit, to the borders of a fresh-water pond, about a mile from the village. After bathing and putting on clean clothes, we would seat ourselves under the shade of a beautiful pine, while I read some chapters in the Bible and the prayers appointed by our Church for the day, ending our devotions with a fervent prayer to the Almighty that he would deign still to watch over and preserve our lives, rescue us from the hands of the savages, and permit us once more to behold a

Christian land. In this manner were the greater part of our Sundays passed at Nootka. I felt grateful to heaven that, amidst our other sufferings, we were at least allowed the pleasure of offering up our devotions unmolested, for Maquinna, on my explaining to him as well as was in my power the reason of our thus retiring at this time, far from objecting, readily consented to it.

The pond was small, not more than a quarter of a mile in breadth and of no great length, the water being very clear, though not of great depth, and bordered by a beautiful forest of pine, fir, elm, and beech, free from bushes and underwood—a most delightful retreat, which was rendered still more attractive by a great number of birds that frequented it, particularly the humming bird. Thither we used to go to wash our clothes, and felt secure from any intrusion from the natives, as they rarely visited it except for the purpose of cleansing themselves of their paint.

In July we at length thought that the hope of delivery we had so long anxiously indulged was on the point of being gratified. A ship appeared in the offing, but alas, our fond hopes vanished almost as soon as formed. Instead of standing in for the shore, she passed to the northward and soon disappeared.

I shall not attempt to describe our disappointment—my heart sank within me, and I felt as though it was my destiny never more to behold a Christian face. Four days after there occurred a tremendous storm of thunder and lightning, during which the natives manifest great alarm and terror, the whole tribe hurrying to Maquinna's house. Here, instead of keeping within, they seated themselves on the roof amid the severest of the tempest, drumming upon the boards and looking up to heaven, while the king beat the long hollow plank, singing, and as he afterwards told me, begging *Quahootze*, the name they gave to God, not to kill them, in which he was accompanied by the whole tribe. This singing and drumming was continued until the storm abated.

As the summer drew near its close, we began to suffer from the frequent want of food, which was principally owing to Maquinna and the chiefs being out whaling, in which he would not permit Thompson and myself to join, lest we should make

A church would have been a welcome sight for Jewitt and Thompson, who resorted to conducting their own services in the woods. This one at Friendly Cove was built in 1956 and is now a museum, housing many of the area's treasures.

our escape to some of the neighbouring tribes. At these times the women seldom or ever cooked any provision, and we were often hungry, but were sometimes fortunate enough to procure secretly a piece of salmon, some other fish, spawn, or even blubber, which, by boiling in salt water with a few onions and turnips, the remains of the Spanish garden, or young nettles and other herbs, furnished us a delicious repast in private.

In the meantime, we frequently received accounts from the tribes who came to Nootka, both from the north and south, of there being vessels on the coast, and were advised by their chiefs to make our escape, who also promised us their aid and to put us on board. These stories, however, as I afterwards learned, were almost all of them without any foundation, and merely invented by these people with a view to get us into their power in order to make slaves of us themselves, or to sell us to others. But I was still more strongly solicited to leave Nootka by a woman.

This was a Wickanninish princess, a younger sister of Maquinna's wife, who was there on a visit. I had the good fortune, if it may be so called, to become quite a favourite with her. She appeared much interested for me—asked me many questions respecting my country, if I had a mother and sister at home, and if they would not grieve for my absence. Her complexion was fairer than that of the women in general, and her features more regular. She would have been quite handsome had it not been for a defect in one of her eyes, the sight of which had been injured by some accident, the reason, as Maquinna told me, why she had not been married, a defect of this kind being by these savages considered as almost an insuperable objection. She urged me repeatedly to return with her, telling me that the Wickanninish were much better than the Nootkians; that her father would treat me more kindly than Maquinna, give me better food and clothes, and finally put me on board one of my own country vessels. I felt, however, little disposed to accompany her, considering my situation with Maquinna full as eligible as it would be with the Wickanninish, if not better, notwithstanding all she said to the contrary.

On the third of September the whole tribe quitted Nootka, according to their constant practice, in order to pass the autumn and winter at Tahsis and Coopte, the latter lying about 30 miles up the Sound in a deep bay, the navigation of which is very dangerous from the great number of reefs and rocks with which it abounds. On these occasions every thing is taken with them, even the planks of their houses, in order to cover their new dwellings.

To a European, such a removal exhibits a scene quite novel and strange: canoes piled up with boards and boxes, and filled with men, women, and children of all ranks and sizes, making the air resound with their cries and songs. At these times, as well as when they have occasion to go some distance from their houses, the infants are usually suspended across the mother's shoulders in a kind of cradle or hammock, formed of bark, of about six inches in depth, and of the length of the child, by means of a leather band inserted through loops on its edges. This they also keep them in when at home in order to preserve them in a straight position and prevent any distortion of the limbs, most probably a principal cause of these people being so seldom deformed or crooked.

The long boat of our ship having been repaired and furnished with a sail by Thompson, Maquinna gave us the direction of it, we being better acquainted with managing it than his people. After loading her as deep as she could swim, we proceeded in company with them to the north, quitting Nootka with heavy hearts, as we could entertain no hopes of release until our return, no ships ever coming to that part of the coast. Passing Coopte, which is situated on the southern bank, just within the mouth of a small river flowing from the east in a narrow valley at the foot of a mountain, we proceeded about fifteen miles up this stream to Tahsis, between a range of lofty hills on each side, which extend a great distance inland and are covered with the finest forest trees of the country. Immediately on our arrival we all went to work very diligently in covering the houses with the planks we had brought, the frames being ready erected, these people never pretending to remove the timber. In a very short time the work was completed, and we were established in our new residence.

Tahsis is pleasantly situated and in a most secure position from the winter storms, in a small vale or hollow on the south shore, at the foot of a mountain. The spot on which it stands is level and the soil very fine, the country in its vicinity abounding with the most romantic views, charmingly diversified, and fine streams of water falling in beautiful cascades from the mountains. The river at this place is about twenty rods in width, and in its deepest part from nine to twelve feet. This village is the extreme point of navigation, as immediately beyond, the river becomes much more shallow and is broken into rapids and falls. The houses here are placed in a line like those at Nootka, but closer together, the situation being more confined. They are also smaller, in consequence of which we were much crowded and incommoded for room.

The principal object in coming to this place is the facility it affords these people of providing their winter stock of provisions, which consists principally of salmon, and the spawn of that fish; to which may be added herring and sprats, and herring spawn. The latter, however, is always procured by them at Nootka previous to their quitting it. At the seasons of spawning, which are early in the spring and the last of August, they collect a great quantity of pine branches, which they place in different parts of the cove at the depth of about ten feet and secure them by means of heavy stones. On these the herring deposit their spawn in immense quantities. The bushes are then taken up, the spawn stripped from the branches, and after being washed and freed from the pine leaves by the women, is dried and put up in baskets for use. It is considered as their greatest delicacy and eaten both cooked and raw: in the former case, being boiled and eaten with train oil, and in the latter, mixed up with cold water alone.

The salmon are taken at Tahsis, principally in pots or weirs. Their method of taking them in weirs is thus: A pot of twenty feet in length, and from four to five feet diameter at the mouth, is formed of a great number of pine splinters, which are strongly secured an inch and a half from each other, by means of hoops made of flexible twigs, and placed about eight inches apart. At the end it tapers almost to a point, near which is a small wicker door for the purpose of taking out the fish.

This pot or weir is placed at the foot of a fall or rapid where the water is not very deep, and the fish, driven from above with long poles, are intercepted and caught in the weir, from whence they are taken into the canoes. In this manner I have seen more

Jewitt at the forge. The introduction of metal tools and weapons drastically changed the aboriginal way of life, from hunting methods to ornamentation.

than 700 salmon caught in the space of fifteen minutes. I have also sometimes known a few of the striped bass taken in this manner, but rarely.

At such times there is great feasting and merriment among them. The women and female slaves being busily employed in cooking or in curing the fish for their winter stock, which is done by cutting off the heads and tails, splitting them, taking out the backbone, and hanging them up in their houses to dry. They also dry the halibut and cod, but these, instead of curing whole, they cut up into small pieces, for that purpose, and expose to the sun. The spawn of the salmon, which is a principal article of their provision, they take out, and without any other preparation, throw it into their tubs, where they leave it to stand and ferment. Though they frequently eat it fresh, they esteem it much more when it has acquired a strong taste.

One of the greatest favours they can confer on any person is to invite him to eat *quakamiss*, the name they give this food, though scarcely anything can be more repugnant to a European palate than it is in this state. Whenever they took it out of these large receptacles, which they are always careful to fill, such was the stench which it exhaled, on being moved, that it was almost impossible for me to abide it, even after habit had in a great degree dulled the delicacy of my senses. When boiled it became less offensive, though it still retained much of the putrid smell and something of the taste.

Such is the immense quantity of these fish, and they are taken with such facility, that I have known upwards of 2,500 brought into Maquinna's house at once, and at one of their great feasts have seen 100 or more cooked in one of their largest tubs.

I used frequently to go out with Maquinna upon these fishing parties and was always sure to receive a handsome present of salmon, which I had the privilege of calling mine. I also went with him several times in a canoe to strike the salmon, which I have attempted to do myself, but could never succeed, it requiring a degree of adroitness that I did not possess. I was also permitted to go out with a gun and was several times very successful in shooting wild ducks and teal, which are very numerous here, though rather shy. These they cooked in their usual manner, by boiling, without any further dressing than skinning them.

In many respects, however, our situation was less pleasant here than at Nootka. We were more incommoded for room, the houses not being so spacious nor so well arranged, and as it was colder, we were compelled to be much more within doors. We, however, did not neglect on Sundays, when the weather would admit, to retire into the woods, and by the side of some stream, after bathing, return our thanks to God for preserving us and offer up to him our customary devotions. I was, however, very apprehensive, soon after our arrival at this place, that I should be deprived of the satisfaction of keeping my journal. Maquinna, one day observing me writing in it, enquired of me what I was doing. When I endeavoured to explain it, by telling him that I was keeping an account of the weather, he said it was not so and that I was speaking bad about him and telling how he had taken our ship and killed the crew, so as to inform my countrymen, and that if he ever saw me writing in it again, he would throw it into the fire. I was much rejoiced that he did no more than threaten, and became very cautious afterwards not to let him see me write.

Not long after, I finished some daggers for him, which I polished highly. These pleased him much, and he gave me directions to make a *cheetoolth*, in which I succeeded so far to his satisfaction that he gave me a present of cloth sufficient to make me a complete suit of raiment, besides other things. Thompson, also, who had become rather more of a favourite than formerly, since he had made a fine sail for his canoe and some garments for him out of European cloth, about this time completed another, which was thought by the savages a most superb dress.

This was a *kutsack*, or mantle, a fathom square, made entirely of European vest patterns of the gayest colours. These were sewed together in a manner to make the best show, and bound with a deep trimming of the finest otter skin, with which the armholes were also bordered; while the bottom was further embellished with five or six rows of gilt buttons, placed as near as possible to each other. Nothing could exceed the pride of Maquinna when

Friendly Cove in 1798.

he first put on this royal robe, decorated like the coat of Joseph with all the colours of the rainbow, and glittering with the buttons, which as he strutted about made a tinkling, while he repeatedly exclaimed in a transport of exultation, *Kiew shish kutsack—wick kum atack Nootka.* A fine garment—Nootka can't make him.

ten

Motivations for Massacre

Maquinna, who knew that the chiefs of the tribes who came to visit us had endeavoured to persuade me to escape, frequently cautioned me not to listen to them, saying that should I make the attempt and he were to take me, he should certainly put me to death. While here he gave me a book in which I found the names of seven persons belonging to the ship *Manchester* of Philadelphia—Daniel Smith, Lewis Gillon, James Tom, Clark, Johnson, Ben, and Jack. These men, as Maquinna informed me, ran away from the ship and came to him. Six of them soon after went off in the night with an intention to go to the Wickanninish, but were stopped by the Hesquiahts and sent back to him. He ordered them to be put to death. A most cruel death it was, as I was told by one the natives, four men holding one of them on the ground, and forcing open his mouth, while they choked him by ramming stones down his throat. As to Jack the boy, who made no attempt to go off, Maquinna afterwards sold him to the Wickinninish. I was informed by the princess Yuqua that he was quite a small boy, who cried a great deal, being put to hard labour beyond his strength by the natives, cutting wood and bringing water, and that when he heard of the murder of our crew, it had such an effect on him that he fell sick and died shortly after. On learning the melancholy fate of this unfortunate lad, it again awakened in my bosom those feelings that I had experienced at the shocking death of my poor comrades.

The king, finding that I was desirous of learning their language, was much delighted and took great pleasure in conversing with me. On one of these occasions he explained to me his reasons for cutting off our ship, saying that he bore no ill will to my countrymen, but that he had been several times treated very ill by them.

The first injury of which he had cause to complain was done him by a Captain Tawnington, who commanded a schooner which passed a winter at Friendly Cove, where he was well treated by the inhabitants. This man, taking advantage of Maquinna's absence (he had gone to the Wickanninish to procure a wife,) armed himself and crew and entered the house where there were none but women, whom he threw into the greatest consternation, and searching the chests, took away all the skins, of which Maquinna had no less than 40 of the best. About the same time, four of their chiefs were barbarously killed by a Captain Martinez, a Spaniard. Soon after, Captain Hanna of the *Sea Otter,* in consequence of one of the natives having stolen a chisel from the carpenter, fired upon their canoes, which were alongside, and killed upwards of twenty of the natives, of whom several were *Tyees* or chiefs. Maquinna himself, being on board the vessel, in order to escape was obliged to leap from the quarter deck and swim for a long way under water.

These injuries had excited in the breast of Maquinna an ardent desire of revenge, the strongest passion of the savage heart. Though many years had elapsed since their commission, still

Maquinna claimed that the unsuspecting Nuu-chah-nulth population had been mistreated by a succession of visitors, who frequently terrorized the inhabitants of the old villages, shown here in a painting by John Webber from the 1780s.

they were not forgotten, and the want of a favourable opportunity alone prevented him from sooner avenging them. Unfortunately for us, the long-wished-for opportunity at length presented itself in our ship, which Maquinna finding not guarded with the usual vigilance of the North West Traders, and feeling his desire of revenge rekindled by the insult offered by Captain Salter, formed a plan for attacking and, on his return, called a council of his chiefs and communicated it to them, acquainting them with the manner in which he had been treated.

No less desirous of avenging this affront offered their king than the former injuries, they readily agreed to his proposal, which was to go on board without arms as usual, but under different pretexts, in greater numbers, and wait his signal for the moment of attacking their unsuspecting victims. The execution of this scheme, as the reader knows, was unhappily too successful. And here I cannot but indulge a reflection that has frequently occurred to me on the manner in which our people behave toward the natives.

Though they are a thievish race, yet I have no doubt that many of the melancholy disasters have principally arisen from the imprudent conduct of some of the captains and crews of the ships employed in this trade, in exasperating them by insulting, plundering, and even killing them on slight grounds. This, as nothing is more sacred with a savage than the principle of revenge, and no people are so impatient under insult, induces them to wreak their vengeance upon the first vessel or boat's crew that offers, making the innocent too frequently suffer for the wrongs of the guilty, as few of them know to discriminate between persons of the same general appearance, more especially when speaking the same language. And to this cause do I believe must principally be ascribed the sanguinary disposition with

Maquinna is shown here with Callicum, another Mowachaht chief. Maquinna watched as Callicum was slaughtered by a member of Martinez's crew.

which these people are reproached. Maquinna repeatedly told me that it was not his wish to hurt a white man and that he never should have done it, though ever so much in his power, had they not injured him.

Were the commanders of our ships to treat the savages with rather more civility than they sometimes do, I am inclined to think they would find their account in it. Not that I should recommend to them a confidence in the good faith and friendly professions of these people so as in any degree to remit their vigilance, but on the contrary to be strictly on their guard and suffer but a very few of them to come on board the ship, and admit not many of their canoes alongside at a time; a precaution that would have been the means of preventing some of the unfortunate events that have occurred, and if attended to, may in future preserve many a valuable life. Such a regulation too, from what I know of their disposition and wants, would produce no serious difficulty in trading with the savages, and they would soon become perfectly reconciled to it.

eleven

New for Winter: Tahsis and Coopte

A mong the provisions which the Indians procure at Tahsis, I must not omit mentioning a fruit that is very important as forming a great article of their food. This is what is called by them the *yama*, a species of berry that grows in bunches, like currants, upon a bush from two to three feet high, with a large, round and smooth leaf. This berry is black and about the size of a pistol shot, but of rather an oblong shape, and open at the top like the blue whortleberry. The taste is sweet but a little acrid, and when first gathered, if eaten in any great quantity, especially without oil, is apt to produce colics. To procure it, large companies of women go out on the mountains, accompanied by armed men to protect them against wild beasts. Here they frequently remain for several days, kindling a fire at night and sheltering themselves under sheds constructed of boughs. At these parties, they collect great quantities. I have known Maquinna's queen and her women return loaded, bringing with them upwards of twelve bushels. In order to preserve it, it is pressed in the bunches between two planks and dried and put away in baskets for use. It is always eaten with oil.

Of berries of various kinds, such as strawberries, raspberries, blackberries, &c., there are great quantities in the country, of which the natives are very fond, gathering them in their seasons and eating them with oil, but the *yama* is the only one that they preserve.

Fish is, however, their great article of food, as almost all the others, excepting the *yama*, may be considered as accidental. They nevertheless are far from disrelishing meat; for instance, venison and bear's flesh. With regard to the latter, they have a most singular custom, which is that any one who eats of it is obliged to abstain from eating any kind of fresh fish whatever, for the term of two months. They have a superstitious belief that should any of their people, after tasting bear's flesh, eat of fresh salmon, cod, &c., the fish, though at ever so great a distance off, would come to the knowledge of it and be so much offended thereat as not to allow themselves to be taken by any of the inhabitants. This I had an opportunity of observing while at Tahsis, a bear having been killed early in December, of which not more than ten of the natives would eat, being prevented by the prohibition annexed to it, which also was the reason of my comrade and myself not tasting it, on being told by Maquinna the consequence.

As there is something quite curious in their management of this animal when they have killed one, I shall give a description of it. After well cleansing the bear from the dirt and blood with which it is generally covered when killed, it is brought in and seated opposite the king in an upright posture, with a chief's bonnet, wrought in figures, on its head, and its fur powdered over with the white down. A tray of provision is then set before it, and it is invited by words and gestures to eat. This mock

Stinging nettle was used to make nets and fishing lines. Plants were not only important as food, but also served spiritual and medicinal purposes.

The camas bulbs were popular trade items because of the sugars produced when they were cooked.

Dried salal berries (*yama*) were an important part of the winter diet and were the only berries dried for winter reserves.

ceremony over, the reason of which I could never learn, the animal is taken and skinned, and the flesh and entrails boiled up into a soup, no part but the paunch being rejected.

This dressing the bear, as they call it, is an occasion of great rejoicing throughout the village, all the inhabitants being invited to a great feast at the king's house, though but few of them, in consequence of the penalty, will venture to eat of the flesh, but generally content themselves with their favourite dish of herring spawn and water. The feast on this occasion was closed by a dance from Sat-sat-sok-sis, in the manner I have already describ-ed, in the course of which he repeatedly shifted his mask for another of a different form.

A few days after, a second bear was taken like the former, by means of a trap. This I had the curiosity to go and see at the place where it was caught, which was in the following manner: On the edge of a small stream of water in the mountains, which the salmon ascend, and near the spot where the bear is accustomed to watch for them, which is known by its track, a trap or box about the height of a man's head is built of posts and planks with a flat top, on which are laid a number of large stones or rocks. The top and sides are then carefully covered with turf so as to resemble a little mound and wholly to exclude the light, a narrow entrance of the height of the building only being left, just sufficient to admit the head and shoulders of the beast. On the inside, to a large plank that covers the top is suspended by a strong cord a salmon, the plank being left loose so that a forcible pull will bring it down. On coming to its usual haunt, the bear enters the trap and, in endeavouring to pull away the fish, brings down the whole covering with its load of stones upon its head and is almost always crushed to death on the spot, or so wounded as to be unable to escape.

They are always careful to examine these traps every day, in order if a bear be caught to bring it away and cook it immediately. For it is not a little singular that these people will eat no kind of meat that is in the least tainted or not perfectly fresh, while, on the contrary, it is hardly possible for fish to be in too putrid a state for them. I have frequently known them, when a whale has been driven ashore, to bring pieces of it home with them in a state of offensiveness insupportable to anything but a crow, and devour it with high relish, considering it as preferable to that which is fresh.

On the morning of the 13th of December commenced what appeared to us a most singular farce. Apparently without any previous notice, Maquinna discharged a pistol close to his son's ear, who immediately fell down as if killed, upon which all the women of the house set up a most lamentable cry, tearing handfuls of hair from their heads and exclaiming that the prince was dead. At the same time a great number of the inhabitants rushed into the house armed with their daggers, muskets, &c., enquiring the cause of their outcry. These were immediately followed by two others dressed in wolf skins, with masks over their faces representing the head of that animal. The latter came in on their hands and feet in the manner of a beast, and taking up the prince, carried him off upon their backs, retiring in the same manner they entered. We saw nothing more of the ceremony, as Maquinna came to us and, giving us a quantity of dried provision, ordered us to quit the house and not return to the village before the expiration of seven days. If we appeared within that period, he should kill us.

At any other season of the year such an order would by us have been considered as an indulgence, enabling us to pass our time in whatever way we wished. Even now, furnished as we were with sufficient provision for that term, it was not very unpleasant to us, more particularly Thompson who was always desirous to keep as much as possible out of the society and sight of the natives, whom he detested. Taking with us our provisions, a bundle of clothes, and our axes, we obeyed the directions of Maquinna, and withdrew into the woods. Here we built ourselves a cabin to shelter us, with the branches of trees, and keeping up a good fire, secured ourselves pretty well from the cold.

Here we passed the prescribed period of our exile with more content than much of the time while with them, employing the day in reading and praying for our release, or in rambling around and exploring the country, the soil of which we found to be very good, and the face of it beautifully diversified with hills and valleys, refreshed with the finest streams of water, and at night enjoyed comfortable repose upon a bed of soft leaves, with our garments spread over us to protect us from the cold.

At the end of seven days we returned and found several of the people of Ai-tiz-zart with their king, or chief, at Tahsis. He had been invited by Maquinna to attend the close of this

Fish traps were usually twenty feet long and about four feet in diameter. This was an incredibly quick way of fishing, as hundreds of fish could be caught in a matter of minutes.

performance, which I now learn was a celebration, held by them annually in honour of their God, whom they call *Quahootze*, to return him their thanks for his past and implore his future favours. It terminated on the 21st, the day after our return, with a most extraordinary exhibition. Three men, each of whom had two bayonets run through his sides between the ribs, apparently regardless of the pain, traversed the room, backwards and forwards, singing war songs and exulting in this display of firmness.

On the arrival of the 25th we could not but call to mind that this being Christmas, it was in our country a day of the greatest festivity, when our fellow countrymen, assembled in their churches, were celebrating the goodness of God and the praises of the Saviour. What a reverse did our situation offer—captives in a savage land and slaves to a set of ignorant beings unacquainted with religion or humanity. Hardly were we permitted to offer up our devotions by ourselves in the woods, while we felt even grateful for this privilege. Thither with the king's permission we withdrew, and after reading the service appointed for the day, sang the hymn of the Nativity, fervently praying that heaven in its goodness would permit us to celebrate the next festival of this kind in some Christian land.

On our return, in order to conform as much as was in our power to the custom of our country, we were desirous of having a better supper than usual. With this view we bought from one of the natives some dried clams and oil and a root called *kletsup* [Pacific silverweed], which we cooked by steaming and found it very palatable. This root consists of many fibres of about six inches long, and of the size of a crow quill. It is sweet, of an agreeable taste not unlike the *quawnoose,* and it is eaten with oil. The plant that produces it I have never seen. [It grew around present-day Victoria, and Indians traded its dried bulbs up the West Coast of Vancouver Island.]

On the 31st, all the tribe quitted Tahsis for Coopte, where they go to pass the remainder of the winter and complete their fishing, taking everything with them in the same manner as at Nootka. We arrived in a few hours at Coopte, which is about fifteen miles, and immediately set about covering the houses, which was soon completed.

This place, which is their great herring and sprat fishery, stands just within the mouth of the river, on the same side with Tahsis, in a very narrow valley at the foot of a high mountain. Though nearly as secure as Tahsis from the winter storms, it is by no means so pleasantly situated, though to us it was a much more agreeable residence. It brought us nearer Nootka, where we were impatient to return, in hopes of finding some vessel there or hearing of the arrival of one near.

The first snow that fell this season was the day after our arrival, on New Year's; a day that, like Christmas, brought with it painful recollections, but at the same time led us to indulge the hope of a more fortunate year than the last.

Early on the morning of the 7th of January, Maquinna took me with him in his canoe on a visit to Upquesta, chief of the Ai-tiz-zarts, who had invited him to attend an exhibition at his village similar to the one with which he had been entertained at Tahsis. This place is between 20 and 30 miles distant up the sound, and stands on the banks of a small river about the size of that of Coopte, just within its entrance in a valley of much greater extent than that of Tahsis. It consists of fourteen or fifteen houses, built and disposed in the manner of those at Nootka. The tribe, which is considered as tributary to Maquinna, amounts to about 300 warriors, and the inhabitants, both men and women, are among the best looking of any people on the coast.

On our arrival we were received at the shore by the inhabitants, a few of whom were armed with muskets, which they fired with loud shouts and exclamations of *wocash, wocash*.

We were welcomed by the chief's messenger, or master of ceremonies, dressed in his best garments, with his hair powdered with white down, and holding in his hand the *cheetoolth*, the badge of his office. This man preceded us to the chief's house, where he introduced and pointed out to us our respective seats. On entering, the visitors took off their hats, which they always wear on similar occasions, and Maquinna his outer robes, of which he has several on whenever he pays a visit, and seated himself near the chief.

As I was dressed in European clothes I became quite an object of curiosity to these people, very few of whom had ever seen a white man. They crowded around me in numbers, taking hold of my clothes, examining my face, hands and feet, and even opening my mouth to see if I had a tongue, for notwithstanding I had by this time become well acquainted with their language, I preserved the strictest silence, Maquinna on our first landing having enjoined me not to speak until he should direct. Having undergone this examination for some time, Maquinna at length made a sign to me to speak to them. On hearing me address them in their own language, they were greatly astonished and delighted, and told Maquinna that they now perceived that I was a man like themselves, except that I was white and looked like a seal, alluding to my blue jacket and trousers, which they wanted to persuade me to take off, as they did not like their appearance.

Maquinna in the meantime gave an account to the chief of the scheme he had formed for surprising our ship, and the manner in which he and his people had carried it into execution, with such particular and horrid details of that transaction as chilled the blood in my veins. Trays of boiled herring spawn and train oil were soon after brought in and placed before us, neither the chief or any of his people eating at the same time, it being contrary to the ideas of hospitality entertained by these nations to eat any part of the food that is provided for strangers, always waiting until their visitors have finished before they have their own brought in.

The following day closed their festival with an exhibition of a similar kind to that which had been given at Tahsis, but still more cruel, the different tribes appearing on these occasions to endeavour to surpass each other in their proofs of fortitude and endurance of pain. In the morning twenty men entered the chief's house, with each an arrow run through the flesh of his sides and either arm with a cord fastened to the end, which as the performers advanced, singing and boasting, was forcibly drawn back by a person having hold of it. After this performance was closed we returned to Coopte, which we reached at midnight, our men keeping time with their songs to the stroke of their paddles.

The natives now began to take the herring and sprat in immense quantities, with some salmon, and there was nothing but feasting from morning till night. The following is the method they employ to take the herring:

A stick of about seven feet long, two inches broad, and half an inch thick is formed from some hard wood, one side of which is set with sharp teeth, made from whale bone, at about half an inch apart. Provided with this instrument, the fisherman seats himself in the prow of a canoe, which is paddled by another. Whenever he comes to a shoal of herring, which cover the water in great quantities, he strikes it with both hands upon them, and at the same moment turning it up, brings it over the side of the canoe, into which he lets those that are taken drop. It is astonishing to see how many are caught by those who are dexterous at this kind of fishing, as they seldom fail, when the shoals are numerous, of taking as many as ten or twelve at a stroke, and in a very short time will fill a canoe with them. Sprats are likewise caught in a similar manner.

About the beginning of February Maquinna gave a great feast, at which were present not only all the inhabitants, but a hundred from Ai-tiz-zart, and a number from Wickanninish who had been invited to attend it. It is customary with them to give an annual entertainment of this kind, and it is astonishing to see what a quantity of provision is expended, or rather wasted on such an occasion, when they always eat to the greatest excess. It was at this feast that I saw upwards of a hundred salmon cooked in one tub. The whole residence at Coopte presents an almost uninterrupted succession of feasting and gourmandizing. It would seem as if the principal object of these people was to consume their whole stock of provisions before leaving it, trusting entirely to their success in fishing and whaling for a supply at Nootka.

twelve

No Sign of Rescue

On the 25th of February we quitted Coopte and returned to Nootka. With much joy did Thompson and myself again find ourselves in a place where, notwithstanding the melancholy recollections which it excited, we hoped before long to see some vessel arrive to our relief. For this we became the more solicitous as of late we had become much more apprehensive of our safety in consequence of information brought Maquinna a few days before we left Coopte, by some of the Cay-u-quets, that there were twenty ships at the northward preparing to come against him, with an intention of destroying him and his whole tribe for cutting off the *Boston*. This story, which was wholly without foundation and discovered afterwards to have been invented by these people for the purpose of disquieting him, threw him into great alarm. Notwithstanding all I could say to convince him that it was an unfounded report, so great was his jealousy of us, especially after it had been confirmed to him by some others of the same nation, that he treated us with much harshness and kept a very suspicious eye upon us. Nothing indeed could be more unpleasant than our present situation, when I reflected that our lives were altogether dependent on the will of a savage, on whose caprice and suspicions no rational calculation could be made.

Not long after our return, a son of Maquinna's sister, a boy about eleven years old who had been for some time declining, died. Immediately on his death, which was about midnight, all the men and women in the house set up loud cries and shrieks, which awakening Thompson and myself, so disturbed us that we left the house. This lamentation was kept up during the remainder of the night. In the morning a great fire was kindled in which Maquinna burned, in honour of the deceased, ten fathoms of cloth, and buried with him ten fathoms more, eight of *i-whaw*, four prime sea otter skins, and two small trunks containing our unfortunate captain's clothes and watch.

This boy was considered as a *Tyee*, or chief, being the only son of Tootoosch, one of their principal chiefs who had married Maquinna's sister, whence arose this ceremony on his interment, it being an established custom with these people that whenever a chief dies, his most valuable property is burned or buried with him. It is, however, wholly confined to the chiefs, and appears to be a mark of honour appropriate to them. In this instance Maquinna furnished the articles in order that his nephew might have the proper honours rendered him.

Tootoosch, his father, was esteemed the first warrior of the tribe and was one who had been particularly active in the destruction of our ship, having killed two of our poor comrades who were ashore, whose names were Hall and Wood. About the time of our removal to Tahsis, while in the enjoyment of the highest health, he was suddenly seized with a fit of delirium in which he fancied that he saw the ghosts of those two men constantly standing by him and threatening him, so that he would take no food except what was forced into his mouth. A short time before this he had lost a daughter of about fifteen years of age, which afflicted him greatly. Whether his insanity, a disorder very uncommon amongst these savages, no instance of the kind having occurred within the memory of the oldest man amongst them, proceeded from this cause, or whether it was the special interposition of an all-merciful God in our favour, who by this means thought proper to induce these barbarians still further to respect our lives, or whether for hidden purposes the Supreme Disposer of events sometimes permits the spirits of the dead to revisit the world and haunt the murderer, I know not. But his mind from this period until his death, which took place but a few weeks after that of his son, was incessantly occupied with the images of the men whom he had killed. This circumstance made much impression upon the tribe, particularly the chiefs, whose uniform opposition to putting us to death at the various councils that were held on our account I could not but in part attribute to this cause. Maquinna used frequently, in speaking of Tootoosch's sickness, to express much satisfaction that his hands had not been stained with the blood of any of our men.

When Maquinna was first informed by his sister of the strange conduct of her husband, he immediately went to his house, taking us with him; suspecting that his disease had been caused by us, and that the ghosts of our countrymen had been called thither by us to torment him. We found him raving about Hall and Wood, saying that they were *peshak*, that is, bad. Maquinna then placed some provision before him to see if he would eat. On perceiving it, he put forth his hand to take some, but instantly withdrew it with signs of horror, saying that Hall and Wood were there and would not let him eat. Maquinna then, pointing to us, asked if it was not John and Thompson who troubled him. *Wik*, he replied, that is, no, *John kiushish—Thompson kiushish*—John and Thompson are both good. Then turning to me and patting me on the shoulder, he made signs to me to eat. I tried to persuade him that Hall and Wood were not there and that none were near him but ourselves. He said, "I know very well you do not see them, but I do."

At first Maquinna endeavoured to convince him that he saw nothing and to laugh him out of his belief. But finding that all was to no purpose, he at length became serious and asked me if I had ever seen anyone affected in this manner, and what was the matter with him. I gave him to understand, pointing to his head, that his brain was injured and that he did not see things as formerly. Being convinced by Tootoosch's conduct that we had no agency in his indisposition, on our return home Maquinna asked me what was done in my country in similar cases. I told him that such persons were closely confined and sometimes tied up and whipped in order to make them better. After pondering for some time, he said that he should be glad to do anything to relieve him and that he should be whipped, and immediately gave orders to some of his men to go to Tootoosch's house, bind him, and bring him to his in order to undergo the operation.

Thompson was the person selected to administer this remedy, which he undertook very readily, and for that purpose provided himself with a good number of spruce branches with which he whipped him most severely, laying it on with the best will imaginable, while Tootoosch displayed the greatest rage, kicking, spitting, and attempting to bite all who came near him. This was too much for Maquinna who, at length, unable to endure it longer, ordered Thompson to desist and Tootoosch to be carried back, saying that if there was no other way of curing him but by whipping, he must remain mad.

The application of the whip produced no beneficial effect on Tootoosch. He afterwards became still more deranged, in his fits of fury sometimes seizing a club and beating his slaves in a most dreadful manner, and striking and spitting at all who came near him, till at length his wife, no longer daring to remain in the house with him, came with her son to Maquinna's.

The whaling season now commenced. Maquinna was out almost every day in his canoe in pursuit of them, but for a considerable time with no success, one day breaking the staff of his harpoon, another, after having been a long time fast to a whale, the weapon drawing owing to the breaking of the shell which formed its point, with several such like accidents arising from the imperfection of the instrument. At these times he always returned very morose and out of temper, upbraiding his men

The whale hunt. Often the *Tyee* would pray for a whale to wash up onshore. A humpback whale could yield 5,000 litres of oil, which was used like butter is today. It was unusual to bring in more than one whale a year.

with having violated their obligation to continence preparatory to whaling. In this state of ill humour he would give us very little to eat, which, added to the women not cooking when the men are away, reduced us to very low fare.

In consequence of the repeated occurrence of similar accidents, I proposed to Maquinna to make him a harpoon, or foreganger, of steel, which would be less liable to fail him. The idea pleased him, and in a short time I completed one for him, with which he was much delighted and the very next day went out to make trial of it. He succeeded with it in taking a whale.

Great was the joy throughout the village as soon as it was known that the king had secured the whale, by notice from a person stationed at the headland in the offing. All the canoes were immediately launched and, furnished with harpoons and seal skin floats, hastened to assist in buoying it up and in towing it in. The bringing in of this fish exhibited a scene of universal festivity. As soon as the canoes appeared at the mouth of the cove, those on board the canoe singing a song of triumph to a slow air to which they kept time with their paddles, all who were on shore, men, women, and children, mounted the roofs of their houses to congratulate the king on his success, drumming most furiously on the planks and exclaiming *Wocash—wocash Tyee.*

The whale, on being drawn on shore, was immediately cut up and a great feast of the blubber given at Maquinna's house to which all the village were invited, who indemnified themselves for their Lent by eating as usual to excess. I was highly praised for the goodness of my harpoon, and a quantity of blubber was given me, which I was permited to cook as I pleased. This I boiled in salt water with some young nettles and other greens for Thompson and myself. In this way we found it tolerable food.

Their method of procuring the oil is to skim it from the water in which the blubber is boiled and, when cool, to put it up into whale bladders for use. Of these I have seen them so large as, when filled, would require no less than five or six men to carry. Several of the chiefs, among whom were Maquinna's brothers, who after the king has caught the first whale are privileged to take them also, were very desirous, on discovering the superiority of my harpoon, that I should make some for them. But this Maquinna would not permit, reserving for himself this improved weapon. He, however, gave me directions to make a number more for himself, which I executed, and also made him several lances with which he was greatly pleased.

As these people have some very singular observances preparatory to whaling, an account of them will, I presume, not prove uninteresting, especially as it may serve to give a better idea of their manners. A short time before leaving Tahsis, the king makes a point of passing a day alone on the mountain, where he goes very privately early in the morning and does not return till late in the evening. This is done, as I afterwards learned, for the purpose of singing and praying to his God for success in whaling the ensuing season. At Coopte the same ceremony is performed, and at Nootka after the return thither, with still greater solemnity, as for the next two days he appears very thoughtful and gloomy, scarcely speaking to anyone, and observes a most rigid fast.

On these occasions he has always a broad red fillet made of bark bound around his head in token of humiliation, with a large branch of green spruce on the top and his great rattle in his hand. In addition to this, for a week before commencing their whaling both himself and the crew of his canoe observe a fast, eating but very little and going into the water several times in the course of each day to bathe, singing and rubbing their bodies, limbs, and faces with shells and bushes so that on their return I have seen them look as though they had been severely torn with briers. They are likewise obliged to abstain from any commerce with their women for the like period, the latter restriction being considered as indispensable to their success.

Whaling rituals were very elaborate and were constituted of many purification rituals to guarantee safety in the dangerous hunt.

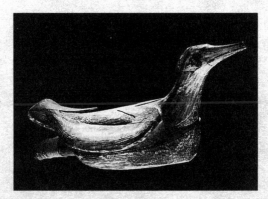

Rattles were almost always in the shape of
birds and used not only for music but also
to communicate with the spirit world.

Early in June Tootoosch, the crazy chief, died. On being
acquainted with his death the whole village, men, women, and
children, set up a loud cry, with every testimony of the greatest
grief, which they continued for more than three hours. As soon
as he was dead, the body, according to their custom, was laid out
on a plank, having the head bound round with a red bark fillet,
which is with them an emblem of mourning and sorrow. After
lying some time in this manner, he was wrapped in an otter skin
robe, and three fathoms of *i-whaw* being put about his neck, he
was placed in a large coffin, or box, about three feet deep, which
was ornamented on the outside with two rows of the small white
shells. In this the most valuable articles of his property were
placed with him, among which were no less than 24 prime sea
otter skins. At night, which is their time for interring the dead,
the coffin was borne by eight men with two poles thrust through
ropes passed around it to the place of burial, accompanied by
his wife and family, with their hair cut short in token of grief, all
the inhabitants joining the procession.

The place of burial was a large cavern on the side of a hill at
a little distance from the village in which, after depositing the
coffin carefully, all the attendants repaired to Maquinna's house.
Here a number of articles belonging to the deceased, consisting
of blankets, pieces of cloth, &c., were burned by a person

appointed by Maquinna for that purpose, dressed and painted in the highest style, with his head covered with white down. As he put in the several pieces, one by one, he poured upon them a quantity of oil to increase the flame, in the intervals between making a speech and playing a variety of buffoon tricks. The whole closed with a feast and dance from Sat-sat-sok-sis, the king's son.

The man who performed the ceremony of burning on this occasion was a very singular character named Kinneclimmets. He was held in high estimation by the king, though only of the common class, probably from his talent for mimicry and buffoonery, and might be considered as a kind of king's jester, or rather as combining in his person the character of a buffoon with that of master of ceremonies and public orator to his majesty. He was the one who at feasts always regulated the place of the guests, delivered speeches on receiving or returning visits, besides amusing the company at all their entertainments with a variety of monkey pranks and antic gestures which appeared to these savages the height of wit and humour, but would be considered as extremely low by the least polished people.

Among those performances that gained him the greatest applause was his talent of eating to excess. I have known him devour at one meal no less than 75 large herring. At another time when a great feast was given by Maquinna, he undertook, after drinking three pints of oil by way of whet, to eat four dried salmon and five quarts of spawn, mixed up with a gallon of train oil, and actually succeeded in swallowing the greater part of this mess, until his stomach became so overloaded as to discharge its contents in the dish. One of his exhibitions, however, had nearly cost him his life. This was on occasion of Kla-quak-ee-na, one of the chiefs, having bought him a new wife, in celebration of which he ran three times through a large fire and burned himself in such a manner that he was not able to stir for more than four weeks. These feats of savage skill were much praised by Maquinna, who never failed to make him a present of cloth, muskets, &c., on such occasions.

Almost all the kings or head chiefs of the principal tribes were accompanied by a similar character, who appeared to be attached to their dignity and are called, in their language, *climmer-habbee*.

This man, Kinneclimmets, was particularly odious to Thompson, who would never join in the laugh at his tricks, but when he began would almost always quit the house with a very surly look and an exclamation of cursed fool! which Maquinna, who thought nothing could equal the cleverness of his *climmer-habbee*, used to remark with much dissatisfaction, asking me why Thompson never laughed, observing that I must have had a very good-tempered woman indeed for my mother, as my father was so very ill-natured a man.

The death of Tootoosch increased still more the disquietude which his delirium had excited among the savages. All those chiefs who had killed our men became much alarmed lest they should be seized with the same disorder and die like him; more particularly as I had told Maquinna that I believed his insanity was a punishment inflicted on him by *Quahootze* for his cruelty in murdering two innocent men who had never injured him.

thirteen

Death—The Captives' Constant Companion

Our situation had now become unpleasant in the extreme. The summer was so far advanced that we nearly despaired of a ship arriving to our relief, and with that expectation, almost relinquished the hope of ever having it in our power to quit this savage land. We were treated, too, with less indulgence than before, both Thompson and myself being obliged, in addition to our other employments, to perform the laborious task of cutting and collecting fuel, which we had to bring on our shoulders from nearly three miles distant, as it consisted wholly of dry trees, all of which near the village had been consumed.

To add to this, we suffered much abuse from the common people who, when Maquinna or some of the chiefs were not present, would insult us, calling us wretched slaves, asking us where was our *Tyee*, or captain, making gestures signifying that his head had been cut off and that they would do the like to us, though they generally took good care at such times to keep well out of Thompson's reach. They had more than once experienced to their cost the strength of his fist. This conduct was not only provoking and grating to our feelings in the highest degree, but it convinced us of the ill disposition of these savages towards us and rendered us fearful lest they might at some time or other persuade or force Maquinna and the chiefs to put us to death.

We were also often brought to great distress for the want of provision, so far as to be reduced to collect a scanty supply of mussels and limpets from the rocks, and sometimes even compelled to part with some of our most necessary articles of clothing in order to purchase food for our subsistence. This was, however, principally owing to the inhabitants themselves experiencing a great scarcity of provisions this season, there having been, in the first place, but very few salmon caught at Friendly Cove, a most unusual circumstance as they generally abound there in the spring, which was by the natives attributed to their having been driven away by the blood of our men who had been thrown into the sea, which, with true savage inconsistency, excited their murmers against Maquinna, who had proposed cutting off our ship. Relying on this supply, they had in the most inconsiderate manner squandered away their winter stock of provisions, so that in a few days after their return it was entirely expended.

Nor were the king and chiefs much more fortunate in their whaling, even after I had furnished Maquinna with the improved weapon for that purpose, but four whales having been taken during the season, which closes the last of May, including one that had been struck by Maquinna and escaped and was afterwards driven on shore about six miles from Nootka in almost a state of putridity. These afforded but a short supply to a population, including all ages and sexes, of no less than 1,500 persons and of a character so very improvident that after feasting most gluttonously whenever a whale was caught, they were several times for a week together reduced to the necessity of eating but once a day, and of collecting cockles and mussels from the rocks for their food.

Even after the cod and halibut fishing commenced in June, in which they met with tolerable success, such was the savage caprice of Maquinna that he would often give us but little to eat, finally ordering us to buy a canoe and fishing implements and go out ourselves and fish, or we should have nothing. To do this we were compelled to part with our great coats, which were not only important to us as garments, but of which we made our beds, spreading them under us when we slept. From our want of skill, however, in this new employ we met with no success, on discovering which Maquinna ordered us to remain at home.

Another thing, which to me in particular proved an almost constant source of vexation and disgust, and which living among them had not in the least reconciled me to, was their extreme filthiness, not only in eating fish, especially the whale, when in a state of offensive putridity, but while at their meals of making a practice of taking the vermin from their heads or clothes and eating them, by turns thrusting their fingers into their hair and into the dish, and spreading their garments over the tubs in which the provision was cooking in order to set in motion their inhabitants. Fortunately for Thompson, he regarded this much less than myself. When I used to point out to him any instances of their filthiness in this respect, he would laugh and reply, "Never mind John, the more good things the better."

Virginia Tom, a Hesquiaht seaweed gatherer.

I must, however, do Maquinna the justice to state that he was much neater both in his person and eating than were the others, as was likewise his queen, owing no doubt to his intercourse with foreigners, which had given him ideas of cleanliness, for I never saw either of them eat any of these animals, but on the contrary they appeared not much to relish this taste in others. Their garments, also, were much cleaner, Maquinna having been accustomed to give his away when they became soiled, till after he discovered that Thompson and myself kept ours clean by washing them, when he used to make Thompson do the same for him.

Yet amidst this state of endurance and disappointment, in hearing repeatedly of the arrival of ships at the north and south, most of which proved to be idle reports, while expectation was almost wearied out in looking for them, we did not wholly despond, relying on the mercy of the Supreme Being, to offer up to whom our devotions on the days appointed for his worship was our chief consolation and support, though we were sometimes obliged by our task-masters to infringe upon the Sabbath, which was to me a source of much regret.

We were, nevertheless, treated at times with much kindness by Maquinna, who would give us plenty of the best that he had to eat and, occasionally, some small present of cloth for a garment, promising me that if any ship should arrive within 100 miles of Nootka, he would send a canoe with a letter from me to the captain so that he might come to our release. These flattering promises and marks of attention were, however, at those times when he thought himself in personal danger from a mutinous spirit—which the scarcity of provision had excited among the natives who, like true savages, imputed all their public calamities, of whatever kind, to the misconduct of their chief—or when he was apprehensive of an attack from some of the other tribes, who were irritated with him for cutting off the *Boston*, as it had prevented ships from coming to trade with them, and who were constantly alarming him with idle stories of vessels that were preparing to come against him and exterminate both him and his people, the Cay-u-quets.

At such times he made us keep guard over him both night and day, armed with cutlasses and pistols, being apparently afraid to trust any of his own men. At one time it was a general revolt of his people that he apprehended—then three of his principal chiefs, among whom was his elder brother, had conspired to take away his life, and at length he fancied that a small party of Kla-oo-quates, between whom and the Nootkians little friendship subsisted, had come to Nootka, under a pretence of trade, for the sole purpose of murdering him and his family, telling us, probably to sharpen our vigilance, that their intention was to kill us likewise.

So strongly were his fears excited on this occasion that he not only ordered us to keep near him armed by day whenever he went out, and to patrol at night before his house while they remained, but to continue the same guard for three days after they were gone, and to fire at one and at four in the morning one of the great guns, to let them know if, as he suspected, they were lurking in the neighbourhood, that he was on his guard.

While he was thus favourably disposed towards us, I took an opportunity to inform him of the ill-treatment that we frequently received from his people, and of the insults that were offered us by some of the stranger tribes in calling us white slaves and loading us with other opprobrious terms.

He was much displeased and said that his subjects should not be allowed to treat us ill, and that if any of the strangers did it, he wished us to punish the offenders with death, at the same time directing us for our security to go constantly armed. This permission was soon improved by Thompson to the best advantage. A few days after, having gone to the pond to wash some of our clothes and a blanket for Maquinna, several Wickanninish who were then at Nootka came thither. Seeing him washing the clothes and the blanket spread upon the grass to dry, they began according to custom to insult him, and one of them, bolder than the others, walked over the blanket.

Thompson was highly incensed and threatened the Indian with death if he repeated the offence. But he, in contempt of the threat, trampled upon the blanket. Drawing his cutlass, without further ceremony Thompson cut off his head, on seeing which, the others ran off at full speed; Thompson then gathering up the clothes and blanket on which were the marks of the Indian's dirty feet, and taking with him the head, returned and informed the king of what had passed, who was much pleased and highly commended his conduct. This had a favourable effect for us, not only on the stranger tribes, but the inhabitants themselves, who treated us afterwards with less disrespect.

fourteen

War

In the latter part of July, Maquinna informed me that he was going to war with the A-y-charts, a tribe living at about 50 miles to the south, on account of some controversy that had arisen the preceding summer, and that I must make a number of daggers for his men and *cheetoolths* for his chiefs. He wished me to make for his own use a weapon of quite a different form, in order to dispatch his enemy by one blow on the head, it being the calculation of these nations on going to war to surprise their adversaries while asleep. This was a steel dagger, or more properly a spike, of about six inches long, made very sharp and set at right angles in an iron handle of fifteen inches long, terminating at the lower end in a crook or turn so as to prevent its being wrenched from the hand, and at the upper, in a round knob or head, from whence the spike protruded. This instrument I polished highly and, the more to please Maquinna, formed on the back of the knob the resemblance of a man's head, with the mouth open, substituting for eyes, black beads, which I fastened in with red sealing wax. This pleased him much and was greatly admired by his chiefs, who wanted me to make similar ones for them. But Maquinna would not suffer it, reserving for himself alone this weapon.

When these people have finally determined on war, they make it an invariable practice for three or four weeks prior to the expedition to go into the water five or six times a day, where they wash and scrub themselves from head to foot with bushes intermixed with briars so that their bodies and faces will often be entirely covered with blood. During this severe exercise they are continually exclaiming, *"Wocash Quahootze, Teechamme ah weith, wik-etish tau-ilth—Kar-sab-matemas—Wik-sish to hauk matemas—I ya-ish kah-shittle—As-smootish warich matemas,"* which signifies, "Good, or great God, let me live—Not be sick— Find the enemy—Not fear him—Find him asleep, and kill a great many of him."

The lake behind Friendly Cove, where purification rituals frequently took place.

During the whole of this period they have no intercourse with their women, and for a week, at least, before setting out abstain from feasting or any kind of merriment, appearing thoughtful, gloomy, and morose, and for the three last days are almost constantly in the water, both day and night, scrubbing and lacerating themselves in a terrible manner. Maquinna, having informed Thompson and myself that he should take us with him, was very solicitous that we should bathe and scrub ourselves in the same way with them, telling me that it would harden our skins so that the weapons of the enemy would not pierce them. But as we felt no great inclination to amuse ourselves in this manner, we declined it.

The expedition consisted of 40 canoes, carrying from ten to twenty men each. Thompson and myself armed ourselves with cutlasses and pistols, but the natives, although they had a plenty of European arms, took with them only their daggers and *cheetoolths*, with a few bows and arrows, the latter being about a yard in length and pointed with copper, mussel shell, or bone. The bows are four feet and a half long, with strings made of whale sinew.

To go to A-y-chart, we ascended from 20 to 30 miles a river about the size of that of Tahsis, the banks of which are high and covered with wood. At midnight we came in sight of the village, which was situated on the west bank near the shore on a steep hill, difficult of access and well calculated for defence. It consisted of fifteen or sixteen houses, smaller than those at Nootka, and built in the same style, but compactly placed. By Maquinna's directions, the attack was deferred until the first appearance of dawn, as he said that was the time when men slept the soundest.

At length, all being ready for the attack, we landed with the greatest silence, and going around so as to come upon the foe in the rear, clambered up the hill. The natives, as is their custom, entered the several huts, creeping on all fours. My comrade and myself stationed ourselves without, to intercept those who should attempt to escape or come to the aid of their friends. I wished, if possible, not to stain my hands in the blood of any fellow creature,

Wars between different aboriginal groups increased after the introduction of the fur trade, as material possessions began to be considered more important.

and though Thompson would gladly have put to death all the savages in the country, he was too brave to think of attacking a sleeping enemy.

Having entered the houses, on the war whoop being given by Maquinna as he seized the head of the chief and gave him the fatal blow, all proceeded to the work of death. The A-y-charts, being thus surprised, were unable to make resistance, and with the exception of a very few, who were so fortunate as to make their escape, were all killed or taken prisoners on condition of becoming slaves to their captors. I also had the good fortune to take four captives, whom Maquinna, as a favour, permitted me to consider as mine and occasionally employ them in fishing for me. As for Thompson, who thirsted for revenge, he had no wish to take any prisoners, but with his cutlass, the only weapon he would employ against them, succeeded in killing seven stout fellows who came to attack him, an act which obtained him great credit with Maquinna and the chiefs, who after this held him in much higher estimation and gave him the appellation of Chehiel-suma-har, it being the name of a very celebrated warrior of their nation in ancient times, whose exploits were the constant theme of their praise.

After having put to death all the old and infirm of either sex, as is the barbarous practice of these people, and destroyed the buildings, we re-embarked with our booty in our canoes for Nootka. Here we were received with great demonstrations of joy by the women and children, accompanying our war song with a most furious drumming on the houses. The next day a great feast was given by Maquinna in celebration of his victory, which was terminated as usual with a dance by Sat-sat-sok-sis.

Repeated applications had been made to Maquinna by a number of kings or chiefs to purchase me, especially after he had showed them the harpoon I had made for him, which he took much pride in, but he constantly refused to part with me on any terms. Among these, the king of the Wickanninish was particularly solicitous to obtain me, having twice applied to Maquinna for that purpose, once in a very formal manner by sending his messenger with four canoes, who, as he approached the shore, decorated in their highest style, with the white down on his head, &c., declared that he came to buy Tooteyoohannis, the name by which I was known to them, for his master, and that he had brought for that purpose four young male slaves, two highly ornamented canoes, such a number of skins of the *metamelth* and of the *quartlack*, or sea otter, and so many fathoms of cloth and of *i-whaw*. As he mentioned the different articles, they were pointed out or held up by his attendants. But even this tempting offer had no influence on Maquinna, who in the latter part of the summer was again very strongly urged to sell me by Ulatilla, or as he is generally called, Machee Ulatilla, chief of the Kla-iz-zarts who had come to Nootka on a visit.

A dagger that Jewitt made for Maquinna, now kept at the U'Mista Cultural Museum.

This chief, who could speak tolerable English, had much more the appearance of a civilized man than any of the savages that I saw. He appeared to be about 30, was rather small in his person, but extremely well formed, with a skin almost as fair as that of a European, good features, and a countenance expressive of candour and amiableness, and which was almost always brightened with a smile. He was much neater both in his dress and person than any of the other chiefs, seldom wearing paint except upon his eyebrows, which, after the custom of his country, were plucked out, and a few strips of the *pelpelth* on the lower part of his face.

He always treated me with much kindness, was fond of conversing with me in English and in his own language, asking me many questions relative to my country, its manners, customs, &c., and appeared to take a strong interest in my fate, telling me that if he could persuade Maquinna to part with me, he would put me on board the first ship that came to his country; a promise which, from his subsequent conduct, I have good reason to think he would have performed. My deliverance, at length, from captivity and suffering was, under the favour of divine providence, wholly owing to him, the only letter that ever reached a European or American vessel out of sixteen that I wrote at different times and sent to various parts of the coast, having been delivered by him in person. So much pleased was I with this man's behaviour to me while at Nootka that I made for him a *cheetoolth*, which I burnished highly and engraved with figures; with this he was greatly delighted.

With hearts full of dejection and almost lost to hope, no ship having appeared off Nootka this season, did my companion and myself accompany the tribe on their removal in September to Tahsis, relinquishing in consequence, for six months, even the remotest expectation of relief.

fifteen

Marriage or Death

S oon after our establishment there, Maquinna informed me that he and his chiefs had held council both before and after quitting Nootka. They had determined that I must marry one of their women, urging as a reason to induce me to consent that as there was now no probability of a ship coming to Nootka to release me, that I must consider myself as destined to pass the remainder of my life with them, that the sooner I conformed to their customs the better, and that a wife and family would render me more contented and satisfied with their mode of living.

I remonstrated against this decision, but to no purpose. He told me that should I refuse, both Thompson and myself would be put to death, telling me, however, that if there were none of the women of his tribe that pleased me, he would go with me to some of the other tribes, where he would purchase for me such a

one as I should select. Reduced to this sad extremity, with death
on the one side and matrimony on the other, I thought proper to
choose what appeared to me the least of the two evils and consent to be married, on condition that as I did not fancy any of the
Nootka women, I should be permitted to make choice of one
from some other tribe.

This being settled, the next morning by daylight Maquinna,
with about 50 men in two canoes, set out with me for Ai-tiz-zart,
taking with him a quantity of cloth, a number of muskets, sea
otter skins, &c., for the purchase of my bride. With the aid of
our paddles and sails, being favoured with a fair breeze, we
arrived some time before sun set at the village. Our arrival excited
a general alarm, and the men hastened to the shore, armed with
the weapons of their country, making many warlike demonstrations and displaying much zeal and activity. We in the
meantime remained quietly seated in our canoes, where we
remained for about half an hour, when the messenger of the chief,
dressed in their best manner, came to welcome us and invite us
on shore to eat. We followed him in procession to the chief's
house, Maquinna at our head, taking care to leave a sufficient
number in the boats to protect the property. When we came to
the house we were ushered in with much ceremony, and our
respective seats pointed out to us, mine being next to Maquinna
by his request.

After having been regaled with a feast of herring spawn and
oil, Maquinna asked me if I saw any among the women who were
present that I liked. I immediately pointed out to him a young
girl of about seventeen, the daughter of Upquesta, the chief,
who was sitting near him by her mother. On this Maquinna,
making a sign to his men, arose and, taking me by the hand,
walked into the middle of the room and sent off two of his men to
bring the boxes containing the presents from the canoes. In the
meantime Kinneclimmets, the master of ceremonies whom I have
already spoken of, made himself ready for the part he was to act
by powdering his hair with the white down.

When the chests were brought in, specimens of the several
articles were taken out and showed by our men, one of whom

Marriages were arranged by parents. Polygyny (having more than one wife or female mate) was allowed only among the chiefs. Divorce was a common phenomenon, especially if the marriage did not yield children.

held up a musket, another a skin, a third a piece of cloth, &c. On this Kinneclimmets stepped forward and, addressing the chief, informed him that all these belonged to me, mentioning the number of each kind, and that they were offered him for the purchase of his daughter Eu-stoch-ee-exqua, as a wife for me. As he said this, the men who held up the various articles walked up to the chief, and with a very stern and morose look, the complimentary one on these occasions, threw them at his feet. Immediately on which all the tribe, both men and women who were assembled on this occasion, set up a cry of *Klack-ko-Tyee*, that is, Thank you, chief.

His men, after this ceremony, having returned to their places, Maquinna rose, and in a speech of more than half an hour said much in my praise to the Ai-tiz-zart chief, telling him that I was as good a man as themselves, differing from them only in being white, and that I was besides acquainted with many things of which they were ignorant. I knew how to make daggers, *cheetoolths*, and harpoons and was a very valuable person whom he was determined to keep always with him, praising me at the same time for the goodness of my temper and the manner in which I had conducted since I had been with them, observing that all the people of Nootka, and even the children, loved me.

While Maquinna was speaking, his master of ceremonies was continually skipping about, making the most extravagant gestures and exclaiming *wocash*. When he had ceased, the Ai-tiz-zart chief arose amidst the acclamations of his people, and began with setting forth the many good qualities and accomplishments of his daughter, that he loved her greatly, and as she was his only one, he could not think of parting with her. He spoke in this manner for some time, but finally concluded by consenting to the proposed union, requesting that she might be well used and kindly treated by her husband. At the close of this speech, when the chief began to manifest a disposition to consent to our union, Kinneclimmets again began to call out as loud as he could bawl, *wocash*, cutting a thousand capers and spinning himself around on his heel like a top.

When Upquesta had finished his speech, he directed his people to carry back the presents which Maquinna had given him to me, together with two young male slaves to assist me in fishing. These, after having been placed before me, were by Maquinna's men taken on board the canoes. This ceremony being over, we were invited by one of the principal chiefs to a feast, at his house, of *klussamit*, or dried herring. After the eating was over, Kinneclimmets amused the company very highly with his tricks. The evening's entertainment was closed by a new war song from our men, and one in return from the Ai-tiz-zarts, accompanied with expressive gestures and wielding of their weapons.

After this, our company returned to lodge at Upquesta's, except a few who were left on board the canoes to watch the property. In the morning I received from the chief his daughter, with an earnest request that I would use her well, which I promised him when taking leave of her parents. She accompanied me with apparent satisfaction on board the canoe.

The wind being ahead, the natives were obliged to have recourse to their paddles, accompanying them with their songs, interspersed with the witticisms and buffoonery of Kinneclimmets. In his capacity of king's steersman, one of his functions which I forgot to enumerate, he not only guided the course of the canoe, but regulated the singing of the boatmen. At about five in the morning we reached Tahsis, where we found all the inhabitants collected on the shore to receive us. We were welcomed with loud shouts of joy and exclamations of *wocash*, and the women, taking my bride under their charge, conducted her to Maquinna's house to be kept with them for ten days, it being a universal custom, as Maquinna informed me, that no intercourse should take place between the new married pair during that period. At night Maquinna gave a great feast, which was succeeded by a dance in which all the women joined. Thus ended the festivities of my marriage.

The term of my restriction over, Maquinna assigned me as an apartment the space in the upper part of his house between him and his elder brother, whose room was opposite. Here I established myself with my family, consisting of myself and wife, Thompson, and the little Sat-sat-sok-sis, who had always been strongly attached to me and now solicited his father to let him live with me, to which he consented.

This boy was handsome, extremely well formed, amiable, and of a pleasant, sprightly disposition. I used to take pleasure in decorating him with rings, bracelets, ear jewels, &c., which I made for him of copper and ornamented and polished them in my best manner. I was also very careful to keep him free from vermin of every kind, washing him and combing his hair every day. These marks of attention were not only very pleasing to the child, who delighted in being kept neat and clean as well as in being dressed off in his finery, but was highly gratifying both to Maquinna and his queen, who used to express much satisfaction at my care of him.

In making my domestic establishment, I determined, as far as possible, to live in a more comfortable and cleanly manner than the others. For this purpose I erected with planks a partition of about three feet high between mine and the adjoining rooms, and made three bedsteads of the same, which I covered with boards, for my family to sleep on, which I found much more comfortable than sleeping on the floor amidst the dirt.

Fortunately, I found my Indian princess both amiable and intelligent for one whose limited sphere of observation must necessarily give rise to but a few ideas. She was extremely ready to agree to anything that I proposed relative to our mode of living, was very attentive in keeping her garments and person neat and clean, and appeared in every respect solicitous to please me. She was, as I have said, about seventeen; her person was small, but well formed, as were her features. Her complexion was, without exception, fairer than any of the women, with considerable colour in her cheeks; her hair long, black, and much softer than is usual with them; and her teeth small, even, and of a dazzling whiteness, while the expression of her countenance indicated sweetness of temper and modesty. She would, indeed, have been considered as very pretty in any country and, excepting Maquinna's queen, was by far the handsomest of any of their women.

With a partner possessing so many attractions, many may be apt to conclude that I must have found myself happy, at least comparatively so. But far otherwise was it with me. A compulsory marriage with the most beautiful and accomplished person in the world can never prove a source of real happiness. In my situation, I could not but view this connection as a chain that was to bind me down to this savage land and prevent my ever again seeing a civilized country. Especially when, a few days after, Maquinna informed me that there had been a meeting of his chiefs in which it was determined that as I had married one of their women, I must be considered as one of them and conform to their customs. In future, neither myself nor Thompson should wear our European clothes, but dress in *kutsacks* like themselves.

This order was to me most painful. But I persuaded Maquinna, at length, so far to relax it as to permit me to wear those I had at present, which were almost worn out, and not to compel Thompson to change his dress, observing that as he was an old man, such a change would cause his death.

Their religious celebration, which the last year took place in December, was in this commenced on the 15th of November and continued for fourteen days. As I was now considered as one of them, instead of being ordered to the woods, Maquinna directed Thompson and myself to remain and pray with them to *Quahootze* to be good to them and thank him for what he had done. It was opened in much the same manner as the former. After which, all the men and women in the village assembled at Maquinna's house in their plainest dresses and without any kind of ornaments about them, having their heads bound around with the red fillet, a token of dejection and humiliation, and their countenances expressive of seriousness and melancholy.

The performances during the continuance of this celebration consisted almost wholly in singing a number of songs to mournful airs, the king regulating the time by beating on his hollow plank or drum, accompanied by one of his chiefs, seated near him with the great rattle. In the meantime, they eat but seldom and then very little, retiring to sleep late and rising at the first appearance of dawn, and even interrupting this short period of repose by getting up at midnight and singing. It was terminated by an exhibition of a similar character to the one of the last year, but still more cruel. A boy of twelve years old with six bayonets run into his flesh, one through each arm and thigh and through each side close to the ribs, was carried around the room, suspended upon them, without manifesting any symptoms of pain.

Maquinna, on my enquiring the reason of this display, informed me that it was an ancient custom of his nation to sacrifice a man at the close of this solemnity in honour of their God, but that his father had abolished it and substituted this in its place. The whole closed on the evening of the 29th with a great feast of salmon spawn and oil, at which the natives, as usual, made up for their late abstinence.

A few days after, a circumstance occurred which, from its singularity, I cannot forbear mentioning. I was sent for by my neighbour, Yealthlower, the king's elder brother, to file his teeth, which operation having performed, he informed me that a new wife, whom he had a little time before purchased, having refused to sleep with him, it was his intention, provided she persisted in her refusal, to bite off her nose. I endeavoured to dissuade him from it but he was determined and, in fact, performed his savage threat that very night, saying that since she would not be his wife, she should not be that of any other, and in the morning sent her back to her father.

This inhuman act did not, however, proceed from any innate cruelty of disposition, or malice, as he was far from being of a barbarous temper. But such is the despotism exercised by these savages over their women that he no doubt considered it as a just punishment for her offence in being so obstinate and perverse. He afterwards told me that in similar cases the husband had a right, with them, to disfigure his wife in this way, or some other, to prevent her ever marrying again.

About the middle of December we left Tahsis for Coopte. As usual at this season we found the herring in great plenty, and here the same scene of riotous feasting as I witnessed the last year was renewed by our improvident natives, who, in addition to their usual fare, had a plentiful supply of wild geese, which were brought us in great quantities by the Hesquiahts.

These, as Maquinna informed me, were caught with nets made from bark, in the fresh waters of that country. Those who take them make choice for that purpose of a dark and rainy night and, with their canoes stuck with lighted torches, proceed with as little noise as possible to the place where the geese are collected, who, dazzled by the light, suffer themselves to be approached very near. Then the net is thrown over them, and in this manner from 50 to 60, or even more, will sometimes be taken at one cast.

On the 15th of January 1805, about midnight, I was thrown into considerable alarm in consequence of an eclipse of the moon, being awakened from my sleep by a great outcry of the inhabitants. On going to discover the cause of this tumult, I found them all out of their houses, bearing lighted torches, singing, and beating upon pieces of plank. When I asked them the reason for this proceeding, they pointed to the moon and said that a great cod-fish was endeavouring to swallow her and that they were driving him away. The origin of this superstition I could not discover.

Though in some respects my situation was rendered more comfortable since my marriage, as I lived in a more cleanly manner and had my food better and more neatly cooked, of which, besides, I had always a plenty, my slaves generally furnishing me, and Upquesta never failing to send me an ample supply by the canoes that came from Ai-tiz-zart; still, from my being obliged at this season of the year to change my accustomed clothing and to dress like the natives, with only a piece of cloth of about two yards long thrown loosely around me, my European clothes having been for some time entirely worn out, I suffered more than I can express from the cold. Especially as I was compelled to perform the laborious task of cutting and bringing the fire wood, which was rendered still more oppressive to me by my comrade, for a considerable part of the winter, not having it in his power to lend me his aid, in consequence of an attack of the rheumatism in one of his knees, with which he suffered for more than four months, two or three weeks of which he was so ill as to be unable to leave the house.

This state of suffering, with the little hope I now had of ever escaping from the savages, began to render my life irksome to me. Still, however, I lost not my confidence in the aid of the Supreme Being to whom, whenever the weather and a suspension from the tasks imposed on me would permit, I never failed regularly, on Sundays, to retire to the woods to worship, taking Thompson with me when he was able to go.

sixteen

Back Again to Nootka

On the 20th of February we returned to our summer quarters at Nootka, but on my part with far different sensations than the last spring, being now almost in despair of any vessel arriving to release us, or of our being permitted to depart if there should. Soon after our return, as preparatory to the whaling season, Maquinna ordered me to make a good number of harpoons for himself and his chiefs, several of which I had completed with some lances when, on the 16th of March, I was taken very ill with a violent colic, caused, I presume, from my having suffered so much from the cold in going without proper clothing. For a number of hours I was in great pain and expected to die, and on its leaving me I was so weak as scarcely to be able to stand, while I had nothing comforting to take, nor any thing to drink but cold water.

On the day following, a slave belonging to Maquinna died and was immediately, as is their custom in such cases, tossed unceremoniously out of doors, from whence he was taken by some others and thrown into the water. The treatment of this poor creature made a melancholy impression upon my mind. I could not but think that such probably would be my fate should I die among these heathen, and so far from receiving a decent burial, that I should not even be allowed the common privilege of having a little earth thrown over my remains.

The feebleness in which the violent attack of my disorder had left me, the dejection I felt at the almost hopelessness of my situation, and the want of warm clothing and proper nursing, though my Indian wife, as far as she knew how, was always ready, and even solicitous, to do every thing for me she could, still kept me very much indisposed, which Maquinna perceiving, he finally told me that if I did not like living with my wife and that was the cause of my being so sad, I might part with her.

This proposal I readily accepted, and the next day Maquinna sent her back to her father. On parting with me she discovered much emotion, begging me that I would suffer her to remain till I had recovered as there was no one who would take such good care of me as herself. But when I told her she must go, for I did not think I should ever recover, which in truth I but little expected, and that her father would take good care of her and treat her much more kindly than Maquinna, she took an affectionate leave, telling me that she hoped I should soon get better, and left her two slaves to take care of me.

Though I rejoiced at her departure, I was greatly affected by the simple expressions of her regard for me and could not but feel strongly interested for this poor girl, who in all her conduct towards me had discovered so much mildness and attention to my wishes. Had it not been that I considered her as an almost insuperable obstacle to my being permitted to leave the country, I should no doubt have felt the deprivation of her society a real loss. After her departure I requested Maquinna that, as I had parted with my wife, he would permit me to resume my European dress. Otherwise, from not having been accustomed to dress like them, I should certainly die. To this he consented, and I once more became comfortably clad.

Change of clothing, but more than all, the hopes which I now began to indulge that in the course of the summer I should be able to escape, in a short time restored me to health. I could again go to work in making harpoons for Maquinna who, probably fearing that he should have to part with me, determined to provide himself with a good stock.

seventeen

Nootka Customs and Traits

I shall not longer detain the reader with a detail of occurrences that intervened between this period and that of my escape which, from that dull uniformity that marks the savage life, would be in a measure but repetitions. Nor will I dwell upon that mental torture I endured from a constant conflict of hope and fear, when the former, almost wearied out with repeated disappointment, offered to our sinking hearts no prospect of release but death, to which we were constantly exposed from the brutal ignorance and savage disposition of the common people. In the various councils that were held this season to determine what to do with us in case of the arrival of a ship, they were almost always for putting us to death, expecting by that means to conceal the murder of our crew and to throw the blame of it on some other tribe. These barbarous sentiments were, however, uniformly opposed by Maquinna and his chiefs, who would not consent to our being injured. But as some of their customs and traits of national character which I think deserving of notice have not been mentioned, I shall proceed to give a brief account of them.

The office of king, or chief, is with those people hereditary, and descends to the eldest son, or in failure of male issue, to the elder brother, who in the regular line is considered as the second person in the kingdom. At feasts, as I have observed, the king is always placed in the highest, or seat of honour, and the chiefs according to their respective ranks, which appear, in general, to be determined by their affinity to the royal family. They are also designated by the embellishments of their mantles, or *kutsacks*. The king, or head *Tyee*, is their leader in war, in the management of which he is perfectly absolute. He is also president of their councils, which are almost always regulated by his opinion. But he has no kind of power over the property of his subjects, nor can he require them to contribute to his wants, being in this respect no more privileged than any other person. He has in common with his chiefs the right of holding slaves, which is not enjoyed by private individuals, a regulation probably arising from their having been originally captives taken in battle, the spoils of war being understood as appertaining to the king, who receives and apportions them among his several chiefs and warriors according to their rank and deserts.

In conformity with this idea, the plunder of the *Boston* was all deposited in Maquinna's house, who distributed part of it among his chiefs according to their respective ranks or degree of favour with him, giving to one, 300 muskets; to another, 150, with other things in like proportion. The king is, however, obliged to support his dignity by making frequent entertainments, and whenever he receives a large supply of provisions he must invite all the men of his tribe to his house to eat it up. Otherwise, as Maquinna told me, he would not be considered as conducting like a *Tyee* and would be no more thought of than a common man.

With regard to their religion, they believe in the existence of a Supreme Being, whom they call *Quahootze*, and who, to use Maquinna's expression, was one great *Tyee* in the sky, who gave them their fish and could take them from them and was the greatest of all kings. Their usual place of worship appeared to be the water, for whenever they bathed they addressed some words in form of prayer to God above, intreating that he would preserve them in health, give them good success in fishing, &c. These prayers were repeated with much more energy on preparing for whaling or for war, as I have already mentioned. Some of them would sometimes go several miles to bathe in order to do it in secret. The reason for this I could never learn, though I am induced to think it was in consequence of some family or private quarrel, and that they did not wish what they said to be heard, while at other times they would repair in the same secret manner to the woods, to pray. This was more particularly the case with the women, who might also have been prompted by a sentiment of decency, to retire for the purpose of bathing, as they are remarkably modest.

I once found one of our women more than two miles from the village, on her knees in the woods, with her eyes shut and her face turned towards heaven, uttering words in a lamentable tone, among which I distinctly heard *Wocash Ah-welth,* meaning "good Lord," and which has nearly the same signification with *Quahootze.* Though I came very near her, she appeared not to notice me but continued her devotions. I have frequently seen the women go alone into the woods, evidently for the purpose of addressing themselves to a superior being, and it was always very perceptible on their return, when they had thus been employed, from their silence and melancholy looks.

They have no belief, however, in a state of future existence, as I discovered in conversation with Maquinna at Tootoosch's death on my attempting to convince him that he still existed and that he would again see him after his death. But he could comprehend nothing of it and, pointing to the ground, said that there was the end of him and that he was like that. Nor do they believe in ghosts, notwithstanding the case of Tootoosch would appear to contradict this assertion, but that was a remarkable instance, and such a one as had never been known to occur before. Yet from the mummeries performed over the sick, it is very apparent that they believe in the agency of spirits, as they attribute disease to some evil one that has entered the body of the patient. Neither have they any priests, unless a kind of conjuror may be so considered, who sings and prays over the sick to drive away the evil spirit.

On the birth of twins they have a most singular custom which, I presume, has its origin in some religious opinion. But what it is, I could never satisfactorily learn. The father is prohibited for the space of two years from eating any kind of meat or fresh fish, during which time he does no kind of labour whatever, being supplied with what he has occasion for from the tribe. In the meantime he and his wife, who is also obliged to conform to the same abstinence, with their children, live entirely separate from the others, a small hut being built for their accommodation. He is never invited to any of the feasts, except such as consist wholly of dried provision, where he is treated with great respect and seated among the chiefs, though no more himself than a private individual.

Such births are very rare among them. An instance of the kind, however, occurred while I was at Tahsis the last time, but it was the only one known since the reign of the former king. The father always appeared very thoughtful and gloomy, never associated with the other inhabitants, and was at none of the feasts but such as were entirely of dried provision. Of this, he ate not to excess and constantly retired before the amusements commenced. His dress was very plain and he wore around his head the red fillet of bark, the symbol of mourning and devotion. It was his daily practice to repair to the mountain with a chief's rattle in his hand, to sing and pray, as Maquinna informed me, for the fish to come into their waters. When not thus employed, he kept continually at home, except when sent for to sing and perform his ceremonies over the sick, being considered as a sacred character and one much in favour with their gods.

These people are remarkably healthful and live to a very advanced age, having quite a youthful appearance for their years. They have scarcely any disease but the colic, their remedy for which is friction, a person rubbing the bowels of the sick violently until the pain has subsided, while the conjuror, or holy man, is employed in the meantime in making his gestures, singing, and repeating certain words, and blowing off the evil spirit when the patient is wrapped up in a bear skin in order to produce perspiration.

Their cure for the rheumatism or similar pains, which I saw applied by Maquinna in the case of Thompson, to whom it gave relief, is by cutting or scarifying the part affected. In dressing wounds, they simply wash them with salt water and bind them up with a strip of cloth or the bark of a tree. They are, however, very expert and successful in the cure of fractured or dislocated limbs, reducing them very dexterously, and after binding them up with bark, supporting them with blocks of wood so as to preserve their position. During the whole time I was among them, but five natural deaths occurred: Tootoosch and his two children, an infant son of Maquinna, and the slave whom I have mentioned, a circumstance not a little remarkable in a population of about 1,500. As respects childbirth, so light do they make of it that I have seen their women the day after, employed as usual, as if little or nothing had happened.

The Nootkians in their conduct towards each other are in general pacific and inoffensive and appear by no means an ill-tempered race. I do not recollect any instance of a violent

The practice of ground burials didn't come to Friendly Cove until much later. The Nuu-chah-nulth custom was generally to be "buried" at sea.

After trade with Europeans provided the Nuu-chah-nulth with finer metal tools, totem poles began to be more elaborate and soon became a collector's item among foreigners. However, when Cook first arrived in the area, there were no totem poles.

quarrel between any of the men, or the men and their wives, while I was with them, that of Yealthlower excepted. But when they are in the least offended, they appear to be in the most violent rage, acting like so many maniacs, foaming at the mouth, kicking and spitting most furiously. But this is rather a fashion with them than a demonstration of malignity, as in their public speeches they use the same violence. He is esteemed the greatest orator who bawls the loudest, stamps, tosses himself about, foams, and spits the most.

In speaking of their regulations, I have omitted mentioning that, on attaining the age of seventeen, the eldest son of a chief is considered as a chief himself, and that whenever the father makes a present, it is always done in the name of his eldest son, or if he has none, in that of his daughter. The chiefs frequently purchase their wives at the age of eight or ten to prevent their being engaged by others, though they do not take them from their parents until they are sixteen.

With regard to climate, the greater part of the spring, summer, and autumn is very pleasant, the weather being at no time oppressively hot and the winters uncommonly mild for so high a latitude, at least as far as my experience went. At Tahsis and Coopte, where we passed the coldest part of the season, the winter did not set in till late in December, nor have I ever known the ice, even on the freshwater ponds, more than two or three inches in thickness, or a snow exceeding four inches in depth. But what is wanting in snow is amply made up in rain. I have frequently known it during the winter months to rain almost incessantly for five or six days in succession.

It was now past mid-summer, and the hopes we had indulged of our release became daily more faint. Though we had heard of no less than seven vessels on the coast, yet none appeared inclined to venture to Nootka. The destruction of the *Boston*, the largest, strongest, and best-equipped ship with much the most valuable cargo of any that had ever been fitted out for the Northwest trade, had inspired the commanders of others with a general dread of coming thither lest they should share the same fate. Though in the letters I wrote imploring those who should receive them to come to the relief of two unfortunate Christians who were suffering among heathen, I stated the cause of the *Boston's* capture and that there was not the least danger in coming to Nootka, provided they would follow the directions I laid down; still I felt very little encouragement that any of these letters would come to hand, when on the morning of the 19th of July, a day that will be ever held by me in grateful remembrance of the mercies of God, while I was employed with Thompson in forging daggers for the king, my ears were saluted with the joyful sound of three cannon and the cries of the inhabitants exclaiming, *Weena, weena—mamethlee*—that is, strangers—white men.

eighteen

Rescue at Hand

S oon after, several of our people came running into the house to inform me that a vessel under full sail was coming into the harbour. Though my heart bounded with joy, I repressed my feelings. Affecting to pay no attention to what was said, I told Thompson to be on his guard and not betray any joy, as our release, and perhaps our lives, depended on our conducting ourselves so as to induce the natives to suppose we were not very anxious to leave them.

We continued our works as if nothing had happened. A few minutes after, Maquinna came in and, seeing us at work, appeared much surprised and asked me if I did not know that a vessel had come. I answered in a careless manner that it was nothing to me. "How, John," said he, "you no glad go board."

I replied that I cared very little about it, as I had become reconciled to their manner of living and had no wish to go away. He then told me that he had called a council of his people respecting us, and that we must leave off work and be present at it.

The men having assembled at Maquinna's house, he asked them what was their opinion should be done with Thompson and myself now a vessel had arrived, and whether he had not better go on board himself to make a trade and procure such articles as were wanted. Each one of the tribe who wished gave his opinion. Some were for putting us to death and pretending to the strangers that a different nation had cut off the *Boston*. Others, less barbarous, were for sending us fifteen or twenty miles back into the country until the departure of the vessel. These, however, were the sentiments of the common people. The chiefs opposed our being put to death or injured, and several of them, among the most forward of whom were Yealthlower and the young chief Toowinnakinnish, were for immediately releasing us. But this, if he could avoid it, by no means appeared to accord with Maquinna's wishes.

Having mentioned Toowinnakinnish, I shall briefly observe that he was a young man of about 23 years old, the only son of Toopeeshottee, the oldest and most respected chief of the tribe. His son had always been remarkably kind and friendly to me, and I had in return frequently made for him daggers, *cheetoolths*, and other things, in my best manner. He was one of the handsomest men among them, very amiable, and much milder in his manners than any of the others, as well as neater both in his person and house, at least his apartment, without even excepting Maquinna.

With regard, however, to Maquinna's going on board the vessel, which he discovered a strong inclination to do, there was but one opinion. All remonstrated against it, telling him that the captain would kill him or keep him a prisoner in consequence of his having destroyed our ship. When Maquinna had heard their opinions, he told them that he was not afraid of being hurt from going on board the vessel, but that he would, however, in that respect be guided by John, whom he had always found true. He then turned to me and asked me if I thought there would be any danger in his going on board.

I answered that I was not surprised at the advice his people had given him, unacquainted as they were with the manners of the white men, and judging them by their own. But if they had been with them as much as I had, or even himself, they would think very different. That he had almost always experienced good and civil treatment from them, nor had he any reason to fear the contrary now, as they never attempted to harm those who did not injure them. If he wished to go on board, he might do it, in my opinion, with security. After reflecting a few moments he said, with much apparent satisfaction, that if I would write a letter to the captain, telling him good of him that he had treated Thompson and myself kindly since we had been with him and to use him well, he would go.

It may readily be supposed that I felt much joy at this determination, but knowing that the least incaution might annihilate all my hopes of escape, I was careful not to manifest it and to treat his going or staying as a matter perfectly indifferent to me. I told him that if he wished me to write such a letter I had no objection, as it was the truth, otherwise I could not have done it.

I then proceeded to write the recommendatory letter, which the reader will naturally imagine was of a somewhat different tenor from the one he had required. If deception is in any case warrantable, it was certainly so in a situation like ours, where the only chance of regaining that freedom of which we had been so unjustly deprived depended upon it. I trust that few, even of the most rigid, will condemn me with severity for making use of it on an occasion which afforded me the only hope of ever beholding a Christian country and preserving myself, if not from death, at least from a life of continued suffering.

The letter which I wrote was nearly in the following terms:

To Captain _____,
of the Brig _____,
Nootka, July 19, 1805.

Sir,

THE bearer of this letter is the Indian king by the name of Maquinna. He was the instigator of the capture of the ship Boston, of Boston in North America, John Salter Captain, and of the murder of twenty-five men of her crew, the two only survivors being now on shore — Wherefore I hope you will take care to confine him according to his merits, putting in your dead lights, and keeping so good a watch over him, that he cannot escape from you. By so doing we shall be able to obtain our release in the course of a few hours.

JOHN R. JEWITT, Armourer
of the Boston, for himself and
John Thompson, Sail-maker of said ship.

I have been asked how I dared to write in this manner. My answer is that from my long residence among these people, I knew that I had little to apprehend from their anger on hearing of their king being confined. They knew his life depended upon my release, and they would sooner have given us 500 white men than have had him injured. This will serve to explain the little apprehension I felt at their menaces afterwards, for otherwise, sweet as liberty was to me, I should hardly have ventured on so hazardous an experiment.

On my giving the letter to Maquinna, he asked me to explain it to him. This I did line by line, as he pointed them out with his finger, but in a sense very different from the real, giving him to understand that I had written to the captain that as he had been kind to me since I had been taken by him, that it was my wish that the captain should treat him accordingly and give him what molasses, biscuit, and rum he wanted.

When I had finished, placing his finger in a significant manner on my name at the bottom and eyeing me with a look that seemed to read my inmost thoughts, he said to me, "John, you no lie?"

Never did I undergo such a scrutiny or ever experience greater apprehensions than I felt at that moment when my destiny was suspended on the slightest thread. The least mark of embarrassment on mine, or suspicion of treachery on his part, would probably have rendered my life the sacrifice. Fortunately I was able to preserve my composure, and my being painted in the Indian manner, which Maquinna had since my marriage required of me, prevented any change in my countenance from being noticed.

I replied with considerable promptitude, looking at him in my turn with all the confidence I could muster, "Why do you ask me such a question, *Tyee*? Have you ever known me to lie?"

"No."

"Then how can you suppose I should tell you a lie now, since I have never done it."

As I was speaking, he still continued looking at me with the same piercing eye, but observing nothing to excite his suspicion, he told me that he believed what I said was true and that he would go on board, and gave orders to get ready his canoe. His chiefs again attempted to dissuade him, using every argument for that purpose, while his wives crowded around him, begging him on their knees not to trust himself with the white men. Fortunately for my companion and myself, so strong was his wish of going on board the vessel that he was deaf to their solicitations, and making no other reply to them than, "John no lie," left the house, taking four prime skins with him as a present to the captain.

Scarcely had the canoe put off when he ordered his men to stop and, calling to me, asked me if I did not want to go on board with him. Suspecting this as a question merely intended to ensnare me, I replied that I had no wish to do it, not having any desire to leave them.

nineteen

Maquinna Is the Hostage

On going on board the brig, Maquinna immediately gave his present of skins and my letter to the captain, who on reading it, asked him into the cabin, where he gave him some biscuit and a glass of rum, at the same time privately directing his mate to go forward and return with five or six of the men armed. When they appeared, the captain told Maquinna that he was his prisoner and should continue so until the two men, whom he knew to be on shore, were released, at the same time ordering him to be put in irons and the windows secured, which was instantly done, and a couple of men placed as a guard over him.

Maquinna was greatly surprised and terrified at this reception. He, however, made no attempt to resist, but requested the captain to permit one of his men to come and see him. One of them was accordingly called, and Maquinna said something to him which the captain did not understand, but supposed to be an order to release us. When the man returned to the canoe, it was paddled off with the utmost expedition to the shore. As the canoe approached, the inhabitants, who had all collected upon the beach, manifested some uneasiness at not seeing their king on board. When, on its arrival, they were told that the captain had made him a prisoner and that John had spoke bad about him in a letter, they all, both men and women, set up a loud howl and ran backwards and forwards upon the shore like so many lunatics, scratching their faces and tearing the hair in handfuls from their heads.

After they had beat about in this manner for some time, the men ran to their huts for their weapons, as if preparing to attack an invading enemy, while Maquinna's wives and the rest of the women came around me, and throwing themselves on their knees, begged me with tears to spare his life. Sat-sat-sok-sis, who kept constantly with me, taking me by the hand, wept bitterly and joined his entreaties to theirs, that I would not let the white men kill his father. I told them not to afflict themselves, that Maquinna's life was in no danger, nor would the least harm be done to him.

The men were, however, extremely exasperated with me, more particularly the common people, who came running in the most furious manner towards me, brandishing their weapons and threatening to cut me in pieces no bigger than their thumbnails, while others declared they would burn me alive over a slow fire, suspended by my heels. All this fury, however, caused me but little alarm. I felt convinced they would not dare to execute their threats while the king was on board the brig.

The chiefs took no part in this violent conduct, but came to me and enquired the reason why Maquinna had been thus treated, and if the captain intended to kill him. I told them that if they would silence the people so that I could be heard, I would explain all to them. They immediately put a stop to the noise, when I informed them that the captain, in confining Maquinna, had done it of his own accord, and only in order to make them release Thompson and myself, as he well knew we were with them. If they would do that, their king would receive no injury but be well treated; otherwise he would be kept a prisoner. As many of them did not appear to be satisfied with this and began to repeat their murderous threats—"Kill me," said I to them, "if it is your wish," throwing open the bear skin which I wore, "here is my breast. I am only one among so many and can make no resistance, but unless you wish to see your king hanging by his neck to that pole," pointing to the yard arm of the brig, "and the sailors firing at him with bullets, you will not do it."

"Oh no," was the general cry, "that must never be; but what must we do?"

I told them that their best plan would be to send Thompson on board to desire the captain to use Maquinna well till I was released, which would be soon. This they were perfectly willing to do, and I directed Thompson to go on board. But he objected, saying that he would not leave me alone with the savages. I told him not to be under any fear for me, for that if I could get him off, I could manage well enough for myself, and that I wished him immediately on getting on board the brig to see the captain and request him to keep Maquinna close till I was released, as I was in no danger while he had him safe.

When I saw Thompson off, I asked the natives what they intended to do with me. They said I must talk to the captain again, in another letter, and tell him to let his boat come on shore with Maquinna, and that I should be ready to jump into the boat at the same time Maquinna should jump on shore. I told them that the captain, who knew that they had killed my ship-mates, would never trust his men so near the shore for fear they would kill them, too, as they were so much more numerous; but that if they would select any three of their number to go with me in a canoe, when we came within hail I could desire the captain to send his boat with Maquinna to receive me in exchange for him.

This appeared to please them, and after some whispering among the chiefs—who, from what words I overheard, concluded that if the captain should refuse to send his boat with Maquinna, the three men would have no difficulty in bringing me back with them—they agreed to my proposal and selected three of their stoutest men to convey me. Fortunately, having been for some time accustomed to see me armed, and suspecting no design on my part, they paid no attention to the pistols that I had about me.

As I was going into the canoe, little Sat-sat-sok-sis, who could not bear to part with me, asked me, with an affecting simplicity, since I was going away to leave him, if the white men would not let his father come on shore and not kill him. I told him not to be concerned, for that no one should injure his father. Taking an affectionate leave of me, and again begging me not to let the white men hurt his father, he ran to comfort his mother, who was at a little distance, with the assurances I had given him.

On entering the canoe, I seated myself in the prow facing the three men, having determined if it was practicable, from the moment I found Maquinna was secured, to get on board the vessel before he was released, hoping by that means to be enabled to obtain the restoration of what property belonged to the *Boston* still remaining in the possession of the savages, which I thought, if it could be done, a duty that I owed to the owners.

With feelings of joy impossible to be described did I quit this savage shore, confident now that nothing could thwart my escape or prevent the execution of the plan I had formed, as the men appointed to convey and guard me were armed with nothing but their paddles. As we came within hail of the brig they at once ceased paddling, when, presenting my pistols at them, I ordered them instantly to go on or I would shoot the whole of them. A proceeding so wholly unexpected threw them into great consternation, and resuming their paddles, in a few moments, to my inexpressible delight, I once more found myself alongside a Christian ship, a happiness which I had almost despaired of ever again enjoying.

All the crew crowded to the side to see me as the canoe came up, and manifested much joy at my safety. I immediately leaped on board, where I was welcomed by the captain, Samuel Hill, of the brig *Lydia* of Boston, who congratulated me on my escape. He informed me that he had received my letter off

Kla-iz-zart, from the chief Machee Ulatilla, who came off himself in his canoe to deliver it to him, on which he immediately proceeded hither to aid me.

I returned him my thanks in the best manner I could for his humanity, though I hardly knew what I said, such was the agitated state of my feelings at that moment, with joy for my escape, thankfulness to the Supreme Being who had so mercifully preserved me, and gratitude to those whom he had rendered instrumental in my delivery. I have no doubt that what with my strange dress, being painted with red and black from head to foot, having a bear skin wrapped around me, and my long hair, which I was not allowed to cut, fastened on the top of my head in a large bunch with a sprig of green spruce, I must have appeared more like one deranged than a rational creature. Captain Hill afterwards told me that he never saw any thing in the form of man look so wild as I did when I first came on board.

The captain then asked me into the cabin, where I found Maquinna in irons, with a guard over him. He looked very melancholy, but on seeing me his countenance brightened up and he expressed his pleasure with the welcome of "*Wocash* John."

Taking him by the hand, I asked the captain's permission to take off his irons, assuring him that as I was with him, there was no danger of his being in the least troublesome. He accordingly consented. I felt a sincere pleasure in freeing from fetters a man who, though he had caused the death of my poor comrades, had nevertheless always proved my friend and protector, and whom I had requested to be thus treated only with a view of securing my liberty. Maquinna smiled and appeared much pleased at this mark of attention from me.

When I had freed the king from his irons, Captain Hill wished to learn the particulars of our capture, observing that an account of the destruction of the ship and her crew had been received at Boston before he sailed, but that nothing more was known, except that two of the men were living, for whose rescue the owners had offered a liberal reward. He had been able to get nothing out of the old man, whom the sailors had supplied so plentifully with grog as to bring him too much by the head to give any information.

I gave him a correct statement of the whole proceeding, together with the manner in which my life and that of my comrade had been preserved. On hearing my story, he was greatly irritated against Maquinna and said he ought to be killed. I observed that however ill he might have acted in taking our ship, yet that it would, perhaps, be wrong to judge an uninformed savage with the same severity as a civilized person who had the light of religion and the laws of society to guide him. That Maquinna's conduct in taking our ship arose from an insult that he thought he had received from Captain Salter, and from the unjustifiable conduct of some masters of vessels who had robbed him and without provocation killed a number of his people.

Besides that, a regard for the safety of others ought to prevent his being put to death, as I had lived long enough with these people to know that revenge of an injury is held sacred by them, and that they would not fail to retaliate, should he kill their king, on the first vessel or boat's crew that should give them an opportunity. Though he might consider executing him as but an act of justice, it would probably cost the lives of many Americans.

The captain appeared to be convinced by what I said of the impolicy of taking Maquinna's life, and said that he would leave it wholly with me whether to spare or kill him, as he was resolved to incur no censure in either case. I replied that I most certainly should never take the life of a man who had preserved mine had I no other reason, but as there was some of the *Boston*'s property still remaining on shore, I considered it a duty that I owed to those who were interested in that ship to try to save it for them. With that view I thought it would be well to keep Maquinna on board till it was given up. The captain concurred in this proposal, saying if there was any of the property left, it most certainly ought to be got. During this conversation Maquinna was in great anxiety, as from what English he knew he perfectly comprehended the subject of our deliberation, constantly interrupting me to enquire what we had determined to do with him, what the captain said, if his life would be spared, and if I did not think that Thompson would kill him. I pacified him as well as I was able by telling him that he had nothing to fear from the captain, that he would not be hurt, and that if Thompson wished to kill him, which was very probable, he would not be allowed to do it.

He would then remind me that I was indebted to him for my life and that I ought to do by him as he had done by me. I assured him that such was my intention, and I requested him to remain quiet and not alarm himself, as no harm was intended him. But I found it extremely difficult to convince him of this, as it accorded so little with the ideas of revenge entertained by them. I told him, however, that he must restore all the property still in his possession belonging to the ship. This he was perfectly ready to do, happy to escape on such terms.

But as it was now past five, and too late for the articles to be collected and brought off, I told him that he must content himself to remain on board with me that night, and in the morning he should be set on shore as soon as the things were delivered. To this he agreed, on condition that I would remain with him in the cabin. I then went upon deck, and the canoe that brought me having been sent back, I hailed the inhabitants and told them that their king had agreed to stay on board till the next day, when he would return, but that no canoes must attempt to come near the vessel during the night, as they would be fired upon. They answered, *woho, woho*—very well, very well.

I then returned to Maquinna, but so great were his terrors that he would not allow me to sleep, constantly disturbing me with his questions, and repeating, "John, you know when you was alone, and more than 500 men were your enemies, I was your friend and prevented them from putting you and Thompson to death, and now I am in the power of your friends, you ought to do the same by me." I assured him that he would be detained on board no longer than the property was released, and that as soon as it was done he would be set at liberty.

At day break I hailed the natives and told them that it was Maquinna's order that they should bring off the cannon and anchors and whatever remained with them of the cargo of the ship. This they set about doing with the utmost expedition, transporting the cannon and anchors by lashing together two of their largest canoes and covering them with planks. In the course of two hours they delivered everything on board that I could recollect, with Thompson's and my chest, containing the papers of the ship, &c.

When everything belonging to the ship had been restored, Maquinna was permitted to return in his canoe, which had been sent for him with a present of what skins he had collected, which were about 60, for the captain, in acknowledgment of his having spared his life and allowed him to depart unhurt. Such was also the transport he felt when Captain Hill came into the cabin and told him that he was at liberty to go, that he threw off his mantle, which consisted of four of the very best skins, and gave it to him as a mark of his gratitude. In return for which the captain presented him with a new great coat and hat, with which he appeared much delighted. The captain then desired me to inform him that he should return to that part of the coast in November, and that he wished him to keep what skins he should get, which he would buy of him. This Maquinna promised, saying to me at the same time, "John, you know I shall be then at Tahsis, but when you come make *pow,* which means fire a gun to let me know, and I will come down."

When he came to the side of the brig, he shook me cordially by the hand and told me that he hoped I would come to see him again in a big ship and bring much plenty of blankets, biscuit, molasses, and rum for him and his son, who loved me a great deal, and that he would keep all the furs he got for me, observing at the same time that he should never more take a letter of recommendation from anyone, or ever trust himself on board a vessel unless I was there. Then grasping both my hands, with much emotion, while the tears trickled down his cheeks, he bade me farewell and stepped into the canoe, which immediately paddled him on shore.

Notwithstanding my joy at my deliverance and the pleasing anticipation I felt of once more beholding a civilized country and again being permitted to offer up my devotions in a Christian church, I could not avoid experiencing a painful sensation on parting with this savage chief, who had preserved my life and in general treated me with kindness and, considering their ideas and manners, much better than could have been expected.

My pleasure was also greatly damped by an unfortunate accident that occurred to Toowinnakinnish. That interesting young chief had come on board in the first canoe in the morning, anxious to see and comfort his king. He was received with much kindness by Captain Hill, from the favourable account I gave of him, and invited to remain on board. As the muskets were delivered, he was in the cabin with Maquinna, where was also the captain, who on receiving them, snapped a number in order to try the locks. Unluckily, one of them happened to be loaded with swan shot, and going off, discharged its contents into the body of poor Toowinnakinnish, who was sitting opposite.

On hearing the report I instantly ran into the cabin, where I found him weltering in his blood, with the captain, who was greatly shocked at the accident, endeavouring to assist him. We raised him up and did everything in our power to aid and comfort him, telling him that we felt much grieved at his misfortune and that it was wholly unintentional. This he told me he was perfectly satisfied of, and while we dressed and bound up his wounds in the best manner we could, he bore the pain with great calmness, and bidding me farewell, was put on board one of the canoes and taken on shore, where after languishing a few days, he expired. To me, his misfortune was a source of much affliction, as he had no share in the massacre of our crew, was of a most amiable character, and had always treated me with the greatest kindness and hospitality.

twenty

Final Escape

The brig being underway immediately on Maquinna's quitting us, we proceeded to the northward, constantly keeping the shore in sight and touching at various places for the purpose of trading.

Having already exceeded the bounds I had prescribed myself, I shall not attempt any account of our voyage upon the coast or a description of the various nations we met with in the course of it, among whom were a people of a very singular appearance, called by the sailors the "Wooden-lips." They have many skins, and the trade is principally managed by their women, who are not only expert in making a bargain, but are as dexterous in the management of their canoes as the men are elsewhere.

After a period of nearly four months from our leaving Nootka, we returned from the northward to Columbia River for the purpose of procuring masts, &c., for our brig, which had suffered considerably in her spars during a gale of wind. We proceeded about ten miles up the river to a small Indian village, where we heard from the inhabitants that Captains Clark and Lewis, from the United States of America, had been there about a fortnight before, on their journey over-land, and had left several medals with them, which they showed us. The river at this place is of considerable breadth, and both sides of it from its entrance are covered with forests of the very finest pine timber, fir, and spruce, interspersed with Indian settlements. Here, after providing ourselves with spars, we sailed for Nootka, where we arrived in the latter part of November. The tribe being absent, the agreed signal was given by firing a cannon. A few hours later, a canoe appeared, which landed at the village and, putting the king on shore, came off to the brig. Enquiry was immediately made by Kinneclimmets, who was one of the three men in the canoe, if John was there, as the king had some skins to sell them if he was.

I then went forward and invited them on board, with which they readily complied, telling me that Maquinna had a number of skins with him, but that he would not come on board unless I would go on shore for him. This I agreed to, provided they would remain in the brig in the meantime. To this they consented, and the captain taking them into the cabin, treated them with bread and molasses. I then went on shore in the canoe, notwithstanding the remonstrances of Thompson and the captain, who though he wanted the skins, advised me by no means to put myself in Maquinna's power. I assured him that I had no fear as long as those men were on board.

As I landed, Maquinna came up and welcomed me with much joy. On enquiring for the men, I told him that they were to remain till my return. "Ah John," said he, "I see you are afraid to trust me, but if they had come with you, I should not have hurt you, though I should have taken good care not to let you go on board of another vessel."

He then took his chest of skins, and stepping into the canoe, I paddled him alongside the brig, where he was received and treated by Captain Hill with the greatest cordiality, who bought of him his skins. He left us much pleased with his reception, enquiring of me how many moons it would be before I should come back again to see him and his son, who had begged him hard to come with him to see me, and saying that he would keep all his furs for me, and that as soon as my son, who was then about five months old, was of a suitable age to take from his mother, he would send for him and take care of him as his own.

As soon as Maquinna had quitted us, we got underway and stood again to the northward. We continued on the coast until the 11th of August 1806, when having completed our trade, we sailed for China, to the great joy of all our crew and particularly so to me. With a degree of satisfaction that I can ill express did I quit a coast to which I was resolved nothing should again tempt me to return. As the tops of the mountains sank in the blue waves of ocean, I seemed to feel my heart lightened of an oppressive load.

We had a prosperous passage to China, arriving at Macao in December, from whence the brig proceeded to Canton. There I had the good fortune to meet a townsman and an old acquaintance, in the mate of an English East-Indiaman, named John Hill, whose father, a wealthy merchant in Hull in the Baltic trade, was a next-door neighbour to mine. Shortly after our arrival, the captain, being on board the English ship and mentioning his having had the good fortune to liberate two men of the *Boston*'s crew from the savages, and that one of them was named Jewitt, my former acquaintance immediately came on board the brig to see me.

Words can ill express my feelings on seeing him. Circumstanced as I was, among persons who were entire strangers to me, to meet thus in a foreign land with one between whom and myself a considerable intimacy had subsisted was a pleasure that those alone who have been in a similar situation can properly estimate. He appeared on his part no less happy to see me, whom he supposed to be dead, as the account of our capture had been received in England some time before his sailing. All my friends supposed me to have been murdered.

From this young man I received every attention and aid that a feeling heart, interested in the fate of another, could confer. He supplied me with a new suit of clothes and a hat, a small sum of money for my necessary expenses, and a number of little

articles for sea-stores on my voyage to America. I also gave him
a letter for my father, in which I mentioned my wonderful
preservation and escape through the humanity of Captain Hill,
with whom I should return to Boston. This letter he enclosed to
his father by a ship that was just sailing, in consequence of which
it was received much earlier than it otherwise would have been.

We left China in February 1807, and after a pleasant voyage
of 114 days, arrived at Boston. My feelings on once more finding
myself in a Christian country, among a people speaking the same
language with myself, may be more readily conceived than
expressed. In the post office in that place I found a letter for me
from my mother, acknowledging the receipt of mine from China,
expressing the great joy of my family on hearing of my being
alive and well, whom they had for a long time given up for dead,
and requesting me to write to them on receiving her letter, which
I accordingly did. While in Boston I was treated with much
kindness and hospitality by the owners of the ship *Boston*, Messrs.
Francis and Thomas Amery of that place, to whom I feel myself
under great obligations for their goodness to me, and the
assistance which they so readily afforded a stranger in distress.

Afterword

Note: This addition to Jewitt's Narrative was included in Heritage House's previous editions of this Narrative. It was written by Dr. Edmond Meany, Jr., a graduate of the University of Washington, who did extensive research on Jewitt's life after he returned to Boston in 1807. Dr. Meany's comprehensive article appeared in the July 1940 British Columbia Historical Quarterly *and is reprinted here, in shortened form, with permission of the B.C. Provincial Archives.*

The captivity of John R. Jewitt among the Indians of Nootka Sound may have been hardly more spectacular than a number of similar adventures in the eighteenth and early nineteenth centuries. Yet there are few tales of Indian captivities which enjoyed so extensive an audience, for by a combination of timely chance and Jewitt's own restless showmanship his story obtained widespread currency along the eastern seaboard of the United States upon his return to civilization.

Before the year was out, Jewitt saw to it that the details of the captivity were preserved for posterity by publishing *A Journal Kept at Nootka Sound,* purporting to be the exact account which he had kept with such pains during his slavery. Yet almost nothing is known of Jewitt's life for the next few years beyond the fact that on Christmas Day, 1809, he married, this time according to the customs of his own people. His first wife was an Indian girl whom he alleged he had been forced to wed during his captivity. Thenceforward he probably spent at least a portion of his time relating his adventures, and perhaps for a livelihood peddled copies of his *Journal* from town to town, as it is known he did with his later publications.

About 1815, however, Jewitt attracted the attention of Richard Alsop, Hartford merchant, and one of the renowned group of American authors of the time known as the Connecticut Wits. Alsop was one of the few millionaires of his day, and his great means permitted him the leisure to indulge in wide reading and in the polemic literary efforts of the local Federalist party. According to his nephew, Theodore Dwight, writing in 1860, Alsop "had a peculiar taste of adventures," and drew from Jewitt the details of his captivity among the Nootkans. Repeated interviews were necessary to obtain the story, Dwight later remembered, and his uncle encountered difficulties from Jewitt's "small capacity as a narrator," and felt the task would have been much easier had the story teller been a Yankee. Dwight was present at his uncle's house on at least one occasion when Jewitt was there and heard him sing Indian songs learned on the Northwest Coast.

Alsop is recognized as a literary amateur and an "incorrigible imitator of late eighteenth century English modes," and his adaptation of Jewitt's tale is no exception to the rule. For his model in this instance he chose Defoe's *Robinson Crusoe*.

The book which Alsop wrote is, of course, *A Narrative of The Adventures and Sufferings of John R. Jewitt*, the first edition of which was printed at Middletown, Connecticut, in the spring of 1815, by Loomis & Richards. The records of the Clerk of the Court for the District of Connecticut show that Jewitt made application for copyright of the *Narrative* on March 8, 1815.

It is not generally known, however, that on the same day Jewitt staked his personal claim to another production: "The Poor Armourer Boy, A Song."

The song was printed as a broadside, on a long sheet of paper, with a cut at the top depicting "The Ship *Boston* taken by the Savages at Nootka Sound March 22—1803." The cut is identical with the frontispiece in the March 1815 edition of the *Narrative*, and at the bottom of the page is the copyright notice and the name of the printing firm, Loomis & Richards. The song itself is ornately "boxed" and is preceded by the explanation, "Imitated from the *Poor Cabin Boy*, of Dibdin, and adapted to the case of John R. Jewitt, a native of Boston, in Great-Britain, the only survivor of the crew of the ship *Boston*, of Boston in New England, who with the captain and officers were cruelly massacred by the savages on the North-West coast of America."

The authorship of Jewitt's song is unknown. As to the original from which it was imitated, investigation reveals little. The Englishmen, Charles Dibdin and his son, Thomas, were prolific writers of sea songs of the parlour type, which were sung widely in the theatres of the period and had a great following among English-speaking people. Jewitt himself was no doubt familiar with them, and it may be that he mimicked in crude verse a well-known song, hoping to obtain a popularity reflected from the Dibdin name. Jewitt, however, made no definite statement of his authorship upon the broadside itself, and the song seems too good to be the work of the unskilled adventurer. It is possible, moreover, that Alsop, with whom Jewitt had been recently conferring, was prevailed upon to dash off the ditty as a supplement to the *Narrative* which he had just written. The verse hardly reaches the standard of Alsop's poetry, yet it differs in metre and rhyme from the style of Dibdin, and such alterations would require some ability with the tools of the trade. Furthermore, many phrases of the song are enclosed with quotation marks characteristic of the imitative tendency of Alsop. Some substantiation for the claim that Alsop or some other person wrote the song likewise might be derived from Jewitt's use of the word "proprietor" rather than "author" in application for the copyright of the song as well as the *Narrative*.

Jewitt's most important years in the purveyance of his tale seem to have been 1815 through 1817. It is not certain whether

The Poor Armourer Boy

No thrush that e'er pip'd its sweet note from the thorn
Was so gladsome and lively as me,
'Till lur'd by false colours, in life's blooming morn
I tempted my fortune at sea.
My father he wept as his blessing he gave,
When I left him "my time to employ"
In climates remote on the rude ocean wave,
Being but a poor Armourer Boy.

Whilst amidst each new scene these "maxims of old"
Upheld me when grief did oppress;
That a fair reputation is better than gold,
And courage will conquer distress:
"So contented I brav'd the rude storm, dry or wet,
Buoy'd up with hopes" light painted toy,
In thinking that Fortune would certainly yet
Deign to smile on the Armourer Boy.

With our ship, on return, with riches full fraught,
We hop'd soon for Boston to steer,
My heart it with exstacy leap'd at the thought,
"My eyes dropp'd through pleasure a tear."
"But, alas! adverse fate so hard" and untrue
"Did all these gay prospects destroy,"
For burn'd was our ship and murder'd our crew,
And wounded the Armourer Boy.

For a long time in pain and sickness I pin'd,
With no one to feel for my woe,
No mother, my wounds, as she sooth'd me, to bind,
No sister her aid to bestow!
By savages fierce for years held a slave,
Did affliction my poor heart annoy,
Till Hope dropp'd her anchor at last on the grave
As the birth of the Armourer Boy.

From slav'ry escap'd, I, joyful, once more
Hail'd a civiliz'd land, but alone
And a stranger was I on a far-distant shore
From that which my childhood had known.
"If such be life's fate, with emotion I cried,"
Of sorrow so great the alloy;
"Heaven grant that sole blessing that ne'er is denied,"
To the friendless Poor Armourer Boy!

his publications of 1815, the *Narrative* and the song, were distributed through established book dealers. It is recorded, however, that he himself set out in a wagon with copies of the book, to peddle them from town to town. Alsop is said to have regretted his part in the transaction, feeling that Jewitt thereafter "became unsettled in his habits by his wandering life in selling the book." Just how far his journeyings took him is unknown, but he was seen dispensing his book from a one-horse wagon in Philadelphia. Another observer recalled seeing Jewitt with a wheelbarrow of books near the Capital in Albany, the adventurer being readily identified by the large head-scar resulting from his wound during the capture of the ship at Nootka. The few extant letters which Jewitt wrote to his family indicate that he travelled at least as far north as Portland, Maine, as far south as Baltimore, Maryland, and even to Nantucket Island. From his stock he could offer two kinds of merchandise to suit the purses of his customers, the more expensive book and the cheaper broadside souvenir of *The Poor Armourer Boy.*

In all, eighteen editions of the book have appeared in print. Two of these were issued in the British Isles. Of the two latest editions, one was published in 1896 by Clement Wilson, of London, with notes by Robert Brown, and the other is a German edition of 1928. Peter Parley, astute editor and publisher for successive generations of young people, placed the story on the market in his series of Miscellanies under the title *The Captive of Nootka,* as a companion to such well-known works as the stories of La Perouse and Alexander Selkirk. This extensive and long record of publication is adequate testimony to the popularity of the *Narrative.*

The attention aroused by early editions of the *Narrative* no doubt accounts for the interest of the second great literary personage to be attracted by the inherent possibilities of the adventurer's tale. About the time Philadelphia intellectuals were reading the 1817 *Analectic* review, Jewitt was in conference concerning a new venture, the dramatization of his Nootka experience, and in this undertaking it was his good fortune to enlist the services of James Nelson Barker.

Barker enjoyed a varied career. Not only was he a noted biographer and playwright but, in addition, he served as a soldier in the War of 1812 and held office in both the Philadelphia and Federal governments. Many of Barker's plays were performed in the theatres managed by William Burke Wood and William Warren in Washington, Alexandria, Baltimore, and Philadelphia. Historians of the theatre differ as to who took the initiative in proposing to Barker that he exploit the Jewitt theme. One authority contends that Wood and Warren "had the journalistic enterprise to commission Barker"; another investigator believes Jewitt took the lead.

As early as March 10 advance notice was given of the Barker play in an advertisement of the Philadelphia Theatre: "In preparation, a Melo Drama, founded on the interesting narrative of Mr. John Jewitt, called the Armourer's Escape, or Three Years at Nootka, with new scenery, dresses, &c. &c. ..." On March 20 the advertisements became more detailed, stating that the new play would open the next evening, Friday, the 21st. It was to be preceded by a tried and favourite comedy, *The Busy Body*, in accordance with the custom of billing two offerings an evening. The prices were the standard tariffs of the theatre, "Box, 1 dollar —Pit, 75 cents—Gallery, 50 cents." Doors were to be opened at 5:30 and the curtain was to "rise precisely at half after 6 o'clock." Notice was called to the play-bills for further details; but particular attention was directed to the concluding feature of the programme, the rendition of *The Song of the Armourer Boy*, to be sung by Mr. Jewitt himself.

No copy of the play has been discovered, as the only manuscript was taken by Jewitt and has disappeared. Description of the performance itself must then depend in part upon the advertisements already cited, but more upon the "bill," a broadside sheet delineating the play in such detail as to be, in the words of one author, a veritable scenario. Therefore little comment upon the contents of the melodrama is necessary. It will be noted that efforts were made to sketch the narrative accurately, even to the point of a faithful recording of the "costume, manners, ceremonies and superstitions of these extraordinary people," the savages of Nootka Sound. To this end,

Jewitt aided in directing the dancers, and, what is more important still, the adventurer was to take the part of the Armourer. The other principal performers were regular members of the company's troupe, among whom were some of the most prominent actors and actresses of the period, including members of the famous Jefferson family.

It is interesting to speculate upon the manner in which the various and complicated scenes were staged. In particular one wonders about the fourth and fifth scenes of Act I, showing the interior of Maquinna's house, and the Nootkan village during the eclipse of the moon, and the procession and ceremonials of the Indians in Act II. How the audience was able to differentiate between the many tribes represented, and to what degree the showmanship of the day simplified for Philadelphia playgoers the elaborate "Ceremonies of the Bear" and the Nootkan War Dance, are questions open to conjecture. That Jewitt held the centre of the stage as much as possible, and revelled in it, we can be reasonably sure. While he had been actually among the savages, the rigours of his captivity had been somewhat lightened by his cheery disposition and his willingness to recite and sing in his own tongue for the amusement of his captors. Now, on the stage, he entertained the more sophisticated Philadelphians in the language of the Nootkans, for near the end of the play he sang the Indian war song. The final curtain fell as Jewitt concluded singing his *Song of the Armourer Boy*.

The brief theatrical career of John R. Jewitt had its beginning and its climax in *The Armourer's Escape* at the Philadelphia Theatre, but he was to have one more gala appearance before his curious public. There was, in the outskirts of Philadelphia, a summer amusement resort called Vauxhall Garden after its London model. Established in 1813 by John Scotti, Italian perfumer and hairdresser, the park or "circus" had enjoyed several successful seasons before opening again in the summer of 1817. The attractions were equestrian performances, fireworks, songs and speeches by famous celebrities, in addition to refreshments and relief in the cool of the suburbs from the heat of the city. Here we find Jewitt listed among Scotti's offerings.

Nothing is recorded of his performance except the simple fact that he "sung songs dressed in Nootka costume."

Later in the summer Jewitt was ill for eight weeks. "I have had," he wrote, "a complaint in my head attended with a fever which brought me very low." But by October 12, when he signed the letter to his wife, he had recovered his health sufficiently to journey to New York. Apparently the correspondence with Mrs. Jewitt had been enlivened by reference to his experiences with the drama. She had stated that she would rather learn he was a corpse than hear of his "being at the theatre," and he commented with feeling, "That is all nonsense and the State of Connecticut selfconceite, but no more of that I expect to heare enough about it..." Perhaps, before he was done with life, he did "heare enough about it," for Jewitt had essayed a venture on the stage in an era when many people considered a theatrical career far from respectable.

From this time forward, Jewitt's recorded life is less colourful. He probably continued his itinerant existence, sending back to his wife and children in Middletown occasional remittances and bountiful expressions of hope and pious wishes. At long last he returned to Connecticut and permanent rest from his wanderings. He died at Hartford, January 7, 1821. [He was 38.]

If Jewitt was not widely mourned at the time of his death, at least his story kept his memory alive for succeeding generations. One of the two editions of his *Journal* and twelve of the eighteen various editions of the popular *Narrative* were published after 1821. Moreover, looking backward from the vantage point of great distance, we see Jewitt as one of the more picturesque characters of his day. Armourer, adventurer, author, peddler, and showman —these were the pursuits of his lifetime. To two men more skilled in letters than himself he provided inspiration for literary achievement of some merit and considerable interest. To countless persons along the eastern seaboard of the United States be brought knowledge of a far country, a land of savage make-believe. Jewitt's life and achievements thus served as links between the Northwest Coast and the awakening nation across the continent of America.

Bibliography

Harbord, Heather. *Nootka Sound*. Surrey, B.C.: Heritage House, 1996.

Kirk, Ruth. *Wisdom of the Elders*. Toronto: Douglas & McIntyre, 1986.

Mather, Christine. *Native America*. New York: Clarkson Potter, 1990.

Pethick, Derek. *The Nootka Connection: Europe & the Northwest Coast, 1790 – 1795*. Vancouver: Douglas & McIntyre, 1980.

Stewart, Hilary. *The Adventures and Sufferings of John R. Jewitt, Captive of Maquinna*. Vancouver: Douglas & McIntyre, 1987.

Recommended Websites:
"European Exploration on the Northwest Coast." Maritime Museum of B.C. <http:www.mmbc.bc.ca/source/schoolnet/exploration/ee_nwc.html>

Canadian Museum of Civilization. <http:www.cmcc.muse.digital.ca/cmc/cmceng/ghhe5eng.html>

"Natives and the Maritime Fur Trade." <http://www.washington.edu/uwired/outreach/cspn/hstaa432/lesson_5/hstaa432_5.html>

"History of Nootka Sound." <http://www.island.net/_goldriv/history.html>

"The First British Ship on the NW Coast." <http:www.hallman.org/indian/cook.html>

Photo Credits

Index

Other books from Heritage House with links to the
Nuu-chah-nulth people and Nootka Sound area

Glyphs and Gallows
The Rock Art of Clo-oose and the
Wreck of the John Bright

by Peter Johnson

978-1-895811-94-0, $9.95 pb

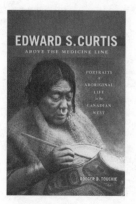

Edward S. Curtis Above the Medicine Line
Aboriginal Life in the Canadian West

by Rodger D. Touchie

978-1-894974-86-8, $19.95 pb
978-1-927051-20-7, $11.99 epub

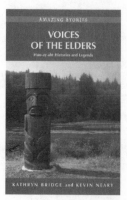

Voices of the Elders
Huu-ay-aht Histories and Legends

by Kathryn Bridge and Kevin Neary

978-1-927051-94-8, $9.95 pb
978-1-925051-95-5, $7.99 epub

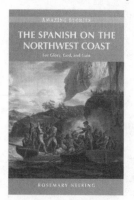

The Spanish on the Northwest Coast
For Glory, God, and Gain

by Rosemary Neering

978-1-927527-83-2, $9.95 pb
978-1-927527-84-9, $7.99 epub

Visit heritagehouse.ca to see more books from Heritage House.